MUSIC LITERATURE OUTLINES

SERIES III

AMERICAN MUSIC FROM 1620-1920

by
HAROLD GLEASON

Graduate Department of Music Literature
Eastman School of Music
of the
University of Rochester

Sole Selling Agent   Levis Music Stores

Rochester 4, New York

PREFACE

These <u>Outlines</u> are intended as a guide to the study of American music from 1620 to about 1920. Each <u>Outline</u> includes a bibliography of books, periodicals and music, and a list of records. The subject of folk music of the North American Indians and Negroes has not been included.

It is the intention of the writer that the <u>Outlines</u> should be supplemented by the books and periodicals listed in the bibliographies. Above all, the student should listen to records with scores and perform the music, whenever possible.

A considerable number of facsimiles of music is included, especially of material that is not readily available. Most of the books from which the facsimiles were made are in the Sibley Music Library of the Eastman School of Music. Acknowledgement is made to the New York Public Library for the facsimiles from the <u>Bay</u> <u>Psalm</u> <u>Book</u> and to The Library of Congress for the facsimile of the original manuscript of "My days have been so wondrous free" by Francis Hopkinson.

The writer wishes to thank Dr. Ruth Watanabe, Librarian of the Sibley Music Library, and Miss Elizabeth Smith for making available valuable material and for help in the preparation of these <u>Outlines</u>.

February 1, 1955   Harold Gleason

Eastman School of Music

Rochester, New York

iii

CONTENTS

ABBREVIATIONS

Books-Periodicals-Music

EAPM	A Program of Early American Piano Music, Howard (VI, 34)
EMCS	A Program of Early and Mid-nineteenth Century Songs, Howard (VI, 34)
EwenMCA	Ewen, Music Comes to America
Hymnal	Hymnal of the Protestant Episcopal Church (1940) (I, 11)
LEAM	Landmarks of Early American Music, Goldman (II, 12)
LU	Liber Usualis
M	Music
ML	Music and Letters
MusAmer	Musical America
MM	Modern Music
MusCour	Musical Courier
MQ	Musical Quarterly
MT	Musical Times
MTNAPro	Music Teachers National Association Proceedings
MWK	The Music That Washington Knew, Fischer (IV, 22)
MWT	The Music of Washington's Time (IV, 21)
Notes	Music Library Association Notes
P	Periodical
PAC	Pioneer American Composers, Milligan (VI, 34)
PMA	Proceedings of the Musical Association
SIM	Sammelbände der Internationalen Musikgesellschaft
YONE	Ye Olde New England Psalm Tunes

Records

A	Album
All	Allegro
ARS	American Recording Society
Art	Artist
Cap	Capitol
CHS	Concert Hall Society
Col	Columbia
Dec	Decca
Clas	Classic
ESM	Eastman School of Music
HSL	Haydn Society
LP	Long playing
Mer	Mercury
Mus Lib	Music Library
New Rec	New Record
R	Record
Sch	Schirmer
Van	Vanguard
Wald	Walden
West	Westminster

Note: The number of the Outline and page of the first entry in the bibliography are given in parentheses.

AMERICAN MUSIC FROM 1620-1920

OUTLINE I

MUSIC IN NEW ENGLAND (1620-1720)

Early Exploration and Settlements in the United States
Music in New England (1620-1720)

I. Early Exploration and Settlements in the United States

A. Spanish
1. Juan Ponce de Leon made the first recorded exploration of the coast of Florida in 1513, landing at St. Augustine. Ferdinando De Soto landed on the west coast of Florida in 1539 and in 1541 marched north and then west to the Mississippi. Coronado came from Mexico as far as the present state of Kansas, and in 1565 the Spaniards explored the Pacific Coast.
a. At the end of the 16th century a small organ is said to have been installed at the Mission of San Felipe in New Mexico, and the Indians were trained to sing here and at other missions in Texas and New Mexico.
2. The Spaniards were not able to keep their settlements on the east coast, however, and at the beginning of the 17th century colonization there was left to the English and Dutch.

B. French
1. The ill-fated Huguenot expeditions, which attempted to settle in Florida in 1562-65, brought the Geneva Psalter of 1562 with them.

C. Dutch and Swedish
1. The Dutch, led by the Englishman, Henry Hudson, discovered the Hudson River in 1609, and a trading post was established at New Amsterdam (New York) in 1613. The surrounding territory was colonized in 1621, but these settlements surrendered to the English in 1664.

D. English
1. Sir Francis Drake explored the California coast in 1579, and there are references to Psalm singing (probably from the Sternhold and Hopkins Psalter of 1562), both aboard ship and on land. Sir Walter Raleigh (1552-1618) attempted to colonize Virginia between 1586 and 1603, and his colony at Roanoke, in what is now North Carolina, was also unsuccessful.
2. The first British settlement in the United States was established at Jamestown, Virginia, in 1607. These settlers, members of the Church of England, also brought with them the Sternhold and Hopkins Psalter and settings by Thomas Est (1592). They developed a plantation colony instead of a commercial-industrial colony as originally planned, and slavery was introduced.

E. Although there are few written records regarding the singing or playing of music, it is obvious that all of the early explorers and settlers used the music of their homeland, if they had time for music at all.

II. Music in New England (1620-1720)

A. The Puritans
1. The history of music in the United States begins with the Puritans in New England.
2. From the time of Queen Elizabeth, the Puritans had opposed the traditional and formal usages of the Church of England and advocated simpler forms of worship.
3. In 1620, a small group (104) of Separatist Puritans sailed from Delftshaven, Holland, stopping at Southampton and Plymouth. They left Plymouth on the "Mayflower" on September 16, 1620 and came to anchor in "Cape Codd" bay on November 21. The coast was explored,

and they decided to land at what is now Plymouth. The first permanent settlement in New England was founded.

   a. Those Puritans, known as Pilgrims, had separated from the Church of England and had become refugees in Holland. They belonged to a group known as Independents (Congregationalists), founded by Robert Browne.

4. The non-Separatist Puritans, who came directly from England, founded the Massachusetts Bay Colony at Boston in 1630.

5. The Puritans were of an entirely different character from the settlers in Virginia. They came to the new country to escape what they considered to be the "sacrilegious rites and discipline" of the Church of England, and they developed an attitude of mind which often led to intolerance.

6. There is evidence that there were many good musicians among the Puritans and some brought instruments to the new country. They were, however, strongly opposed to any music in religious services except the unison singing of metrical Psalms, and these they sang with great enthusiasm.

7. The printing of music was not encouraged, as the Puritans felt it might lead to the playing of instruments (which they associated with ceremonial worship and secular amusements) in church, and also encourage the "vanity" of choir singing. Organs were denounced by John Cotton, Cotton Mather, and other divines and were not allowed in New England churches until 1713 (King's Chapel).

8. Harvard University was founded in New Towne (Cambridge) in 1636 by a grant of the Massachusetts Bay Colony. John Harvard left an endowment to the college in 1639 and it was named for him.

B. Psalters used by the Puritans (1620-1720)

   1. Ainsworth Psalter (1612)

      a. The Book of Psalmes, Englished both in Prose and Metre, known as the Ainsworth Psalter, was prepared by Henry Ainsworth (1571-1622) for the English Separatists in Holland and was published in Amsterdam in 1612. A second edition, The Psalmes in Metre (M 1) appeared in 1618. Ainsworth, a Separatist pastor and distinguished scholar, had fled to Amsterdam in 1593 to escape religious persecution.

      b. The Pilgrims brought the Ainsworth Psalter to America in 1620, and it was used until the adoption of The Bay Psalm Book in 1692 at the time the Plymouth settlement merged with the Massachusetts Bay Colony at Boston.

      c. The original edition (1612) had thirty-nine different tunes for the 150 Psalms. Many tunes had their origin in the Geneva Psalter (1562), although Ainsworth took them from the Sternhold and Hopkins Psalter or the Dutch Psalter.

         1) The Geneva Psalter was translated into Dutch verse in 1566 and was adapted to tunes by Bourgeois in the Geneva Psalter. It became widely used in the Reformed Church throughout the Netherlands and was used at the Collegiate Dutch Church of New York until 1767.

      d. The melodies of the Ainsworth Psalter are printed in single lines with diamond-shaped half and whole notes and without barlines. The C clef is used throughout, generally on the third or fourth line. Psalms 13 and 32 to the C clef on the second line, and Psalm 35 has the C clef on the first line. Time signatures are ₵, except Psalms 42, 45, 50.

      e. There is frequent use of Long Metre (8-8-8-8), which is characteristic of French texts. (The numbers refer to the number of syllables in each of the four lines of the stanzas.)

      f. Nearly one-third of the modes used are Ionian; the remainder are mostly Dorian or Aeolian. The tune for Psalm 89 is half in Ionian on F and half in Dorian on G. A transposition down a fifth with a signature of one flat is frequent.

g. The tune "Old Hundredth," widely sung today, was composed (or adapted from a secular song) by Louis Bourgeois. It first appeared in the Geneva Psalter (1551) set to Psalm 34. The Sternhold and Hopkins Psalter (1561) included the tune set to Psalm 100 as versified by Wm. Kethe. The tune appeared in Lutheran hymnbooks (1562) and in the Ainsworth Psalter and Bay Psalm Book (1698).

h. The tune for Psalm 84, the longest in the Ainsworth Psalter, resembles "Vigiles et Sancti" (Hymnal No. 599).

i. The Puritans sang the Psalms seated, and it was not until the beginning of the 19th century that congregations stood during the singing of metrical Psalms.

j. Music: Hymnal Nos. 147 (Psalm 34), 179 (Psalm 5), 220 (Psalm 124), 278 (Psalm 100), 284 (Psalm 15), 536 (Psalm 8); YONE p. 1; M 1; M 14.

2. Sternhold and Hopkins Psalter

a. The English Psalters had their beginnings with the publication of 19 metrical Psalms by Thomas Sternhold (d. 1549) shortly before 1549, followed by 37 more published posthumously. His work was continued by John Hopkins, who added seven more Psalms which were included in an edition of 1551.

   1) The 150 Psalms were published in Geneva in 1556 for the English and Scottish refugees from the persecutions of the Catholic "Bloody Mary." This edition was reprinted in 1560 and 1561. The latter edition included 25 texts by the exiled Scottish minister, William Kethe.

b. Work on the Sternhold and Hopkins Psalter continued during the reign of Elizabeth, and in 1562 The Whole Booke of Psalms was published by John Day in London. This edition, popularly known as "Sternhold and Hopkins" or sometimes "John Day's Psalter," was widely used by English-speaking Protestants and became the standard form, going through 78 editions before 1600 (See B 4; pp. 16, 17, 18, for examples of the poetry).

c. The Sternhold and Hopkins Psalter was brought to America by the Puritans of the Massachusetts Bay Colony who settled around Boston in 1630.

   1) The Psalter contained 42 tunes, some of which had been used in earlier editions.

   2) Common Metre (8-6-8-6), typical of English tunes, and major-sounding modes are used most frequently. Some tunes came from French sources and others were original compositions.

   3) English tunes are characterized by several shorter notes between two longer ones. Tunes of French origin show more variety in rhythmic patterns.

d. A "New Version of the Psalms" by Nahum Tate (1652-1715), librettist of Purcell's Dido and Aeneas, and Nicholas Brady appeared in 1696 and went through many editions, retaining its popularity until the end of the 18th century. The earlier version of Sternhold and Hopkins was then known as the "Old Version."

   1) The "New Version" included about forty versions by Sternhold, fifty-six by Hopkins, and the remainder by ten other contributors including William Kethe, who had versified Psalm 100 (Hymnal no. 278) in the early edition of 1561.

e. Music: YONE p. 4; Hymnal no. 59 (first half of an eight-line tune set to Psalm 132); Hymnal nos. 13, 85, 390, 439, 450 (texts only); M 16; M 17; M 18; M 19.

3. The Bay Psalm Book (1640)

a. As early as 1636 the Puritan divines began to be dissatisfied with the Sternhold and Hopkins translations of the Psalms. Thirty "pious and learned Ministers" were therefore appointed to translate the Psalms again and set them into verse. Most of the work was done by three men (Robert Mather, Thomas Welde, John Eliot), and the result of their labors was The Bay Psalm Book.

b. The Whole Booke of Psalms Faithfully Translated into English Metre
with a preface by Robert Mather, known as The Bay Psalm Book, was
published by Stephen Daye in Cambridge in 1640 and was the first
book to be printed in America. Only ten copies of the 1700 printed
in the first edition (1640), and two copies of the second edition
(1647), are known. A price of $151,000 was recently paid for a
copy of the first edition.

c. The Bay Psalm Book soon became popular and replaced other Psalters,
except in Ipswich and Salem (until 1667), and the Plymouth Colony
(until 1692). The poor quality of the poetry gradually became
evident, however, and a revised edition, with the addition of a
number of "hymns and spiritual songs," was published in 1651. This
version was in general use for more than 100 years, and a total of
27 editions was printed in New England by 1762.

d. It was reprinted in England as early as 1647, and the revised
version of 1651 (The Psalms, Hymns, and Spiritual Songs of the Old
and New Testament) was followed by over twenty editions by 1754.
It was also reprinted in Scotland several times between 1732 and
1759. A versification of the Psalms in the Algonquin language was
made by John Eliot and printed at Cambridge, Massachusetts, in 1661.

e. The Bay Psalm Book had begun to be considered old-fashioned as
early as 1700, and a half-century later it was replaced by Tate and
Brady's New Version of the Sternhold and Hopkins. About 1800,
other hymn books, particularly Watt's Psalms and Hymns, printed by
Benjamin Franklin in Philadelphia in 1741, became popular.

f. The first edition (1640) had no music, but at the end of the book
was an "Admonition" about the tunes to be used. Most of these
were to be found in Ravenscroft's (1621) or other English Psalters,
principally Sternhold and Hopkins.

g. The ninth edition of The Bay Psalm Book (1698) had thirteen tunes,
the first surviving book with music printed in North America. The
tunes were Oxford, Litchfield, Low-Dutch, York, Windsor, Cambridge,
St. David's, Martyrs, Hackney, 119th Psalm Tune, 100th Psalm Tune,
115th Psalm Tune, 148th Psalm Tune. These tunes were borrowed
from the Ainsworth Psalter, Sternhold and Hopkins Psalter, Ravenscroft's Whole Booke of Psalms (1621), and the Scottish Psalter.

1) The thirteen tunes were printed from wood-cuts in diamond-shape
notes without bar-lines, except at the end of each line of text.
They are set in two-part harmony and are mostly in Common Metre
(8-6-8-6). The tune Cambridge is in Short Metre (6-6-6-6); the
Old Hundredth tune is in Long Metre (8-8-8-8) with another version of the 100th Psalm in Common Metre (8-6-8-6); the 148th
Psalm is in "Hallelujah" Metre (6-6-6-6-4-4-4-4).

2) Music: M 3; M 4; YONE p. 3; Hymnal nos. 278 (Psalm 100), 284
(Windsor), 312 (York), 547 (Martyrs).

h. The lack of instruments and printed music in the churches soon re-
sulted in the practice of "lining-out" the Psalms, a custom which
originated in England. The lining-out was done by a deacon or pre-
centor who read (rarely sang) one or two lines of the Psalm and
then led the singing of what had been read. As early as 1647,
however, the Rev. John Cotton wrote: "that where all have books
and can reade, or else can say the Psalme by heart, it were need-
lesse there to read each line of the Psalme before hand in order
singing." The Psalm tunes were learned by rote, and it was not
until early in the 18th century that an effort was made to teach
people to "sing by note."

4. Part settings of Psalm tunes for use in home singing were made by
many composers, and many of the Pilgrims were said to be "very expert
in music." The tune, in these settings, usually appeared in the
cantus or in the tenor part. In England, settings were made by John
Day (1563), William Damon (1579), Thomas Este (East, Est) (1592),
Thomas Ravenscroft (1621), Henry Lawes (1648), and on the continent

by Bourgeois (1547), Goudimel (1565), Le Jeune (1601), Sweelinck (1604)
and others.
  a. Music: <u>M</u> 2; <u>M</u> 6; <u>M</u> 7; <u>M</u> 8; <u>M</u> 9; <u>M</u> 10; <u>M</u> 12; <u>M</u> 15
    1) Este: <u>Hymnal</u> nos 13, 115
    2) Ravenscroft: <u>Hymnal</u> nos. 7, 260, 297; <u>YONE</u> p. 3
C. Merry Mount
  1. Thomas Morton landed at Plymouth in 1626 and established a colony,
      Merry Mount, nearby. The Puritans and other colonists attempted to
      suppress Morton and his followers because of their Maypole celebrations,
      drinking, and above all, for selling guns and ammunitions to the Ind-
      ians. Hawthorne glamourized happenings at Merry Mount, and his story
      is the basis for the libretto by Richard L. Stokes of Howard Hanson's
      opera, <u>Merry Mount</u>.

BIBLIOGRAPHY

Books

A general reference for American Music is <u>Our American Music</u> by John Tasker
Howard (<u>B</u> 7). Thus book will not be listed in the bibliographies in the following <u>Outlines</u>.

1. Ellinwood, L.   <u>The History of American Church Music</u>. New York: More-
      house-Gorham, 1953. (ML 200 E46)

2. Fisher, W. A.   <u>Notes on Music in Old Boston</u>. Boston: Oliver Ditson
      Co., 1918. (ML 200.8 B7F53)

3. Foote, H. W.   <u>An Account of the Bay Psalm Book</u>. New York: The Hymn
      Society of America, 1940. (ML 3111 F688a)

4. Foote, H. W.   <u>Three Centuries of American Hymnody</u>. Cambridge, Mass.:
      Harvard University Press, 1940. (ML 3111 F688t)

5. Gould, N. D.   <u>History of Church Music in America</u>. Boston: Gould and
      Lincoln, 1853.

6. Hood, G.   <u>A History of Music in New England</u>. Boston: Wilkens,
      Carter and Co., 1846. (ML 200 H77)

7. Howard, J. T.   <u>Our American Music</u>. New York: Thomas Y. Crowell Co.,
      1939. (ML 200 H849)

8. MacDougall, H. C.   <u>Early New England Psalmody</u>. Brattleboro: Stephen Daye
      Press, 1940.

9. Scholes, P. B.   <u>The Puritans and Music in England and New England</u>.
      London: Oxford University Press. H. Milford, 1934. (ML 194 S68P)

10. Stevenson, R. M.   <u>Patterns of Protestant Church Music</u>. Durham, N.C.:
      Duke University Press, 1953. (ML 3100 S948)

11. Stewart, H. W.   <u>The Use of the French Psalm Tune in the Motet from
      1539-1625</u>. ESM Thesis, 1939.

12. Warrington, J.   <u>Short Titles of Books Relating to the History and
      Practice of Psalmody in the U.S. (1620-1860)</u>. Philadelphia: Printed
      privately, 1898. (ML 128 P97W29)

Periodicals

1. Britton, A. P. and I. Lowens. "Unlocated Titles in Early Sacred American Music," <u>Notes</u> XI (1953), 33.

2. McGill, A.   "Old Mission Music," <u>MQ</u> XXIV (1938), 192.

3. Pratt, W. S.   "The Importance of the Early French Psalter," <u>MQ</u> XXI (1935), 25.

4. Truro, The Bishop   "The Rhythm of Metrical Psalm Tunes," <u>ML</u> IX (1928), 29.

5. Woodward, G. R.   "The Genevan Psalter of 1562, Set in Four-Part Harmony by Claude Goudimel, in 1565," PMA XLIV (1917-18), 167.

Music

1. Ainsworth, H.   <u>The Psalmes in Metre</u>, Amsterdam, 1618; <u>Annotations Upon the Book of Psalmes</u>, 2nd ed., 1617; <u>Solomon's Song of Songs</u>, 1623. (M 1490 A297)

2. <u>Ainsworth Psalter, The</u> Psalm 65 with settings by Claude Goudimel. Preface by C. S. Smith. New York: The New York Public Library, 1938. (M 2 A296)

3. <u>Bay Psalm Book, The</u>   Cambridge, Mass.: Stephen Daye, 1640. Facsimile reprint of the first edition. Introduction by Wilberforce Eames. New York: Dodd, Mead, and Company, 1903. (M 2.4 B356)

4. <u>Bay Psalm Book, The</u>   Boston: J. Phillips, 1729. (M 2116 P974B)

5. <u>Calvin's First Psalter</u> Ed. R. R. Terry. London: E. Benn Ltd., 1932. (M 2183.6 C168T)

6. Damon, W.   <u>The former Booke of the Musicke of M. William Damon, late one of her maiesties Musitions</u>. London: T. Este, 1591. Facsimile edition of Cantus, Altus, Tenor, Bassus parts. (M 2.8 D163)

7. Day, J.   <u>Psalms</u>. Tenor, Contra Tenor, Medius, Bassus. London: John Day, 1563. Facsimile reprint of separate parts. (M 218 D274p)

8. Este, T.   <u>The Whole Booke of Psalmes; With Their Wonted Tunes, as they are song in Churches, composed into foure parts</u>. London: Thomas Est, 1592. London: Chappell, 1844. ed. by E. F. Rimbault. (M 2.3 E58M98, vol. 11)

9. Expert, H.   <u>Les Maitres Musiciens de la Renaissance Française</u>, vols. II, IV, VI. Paris: A. Leduc, 1895-1908. (M 2.3 F8E9)

10. Goudimel, C.   <u>Les Psaumes mis en rime françoise</u> (1565), facs. ed. Kassel: Bärenreiter-Verlag, 1935. (M 2.4 B355G68P)

11. <u>Hymnal of the Protestant Episcopal Church</u> (1940). New York: The Church Pension Fund, 1940. <u>The Hymnal 1940 Companion</u>. New York: The Church Pension Fund, 1949. (ML 3166 P967)

12. Lawes, H.   <u>Choice psalms put into Musick, for the Voices</u>. London: James Young, 1648. (M 1490 L417c)

13. Pratt, W. S.   <u>The Music of the French Psalter of 1562</u>. New York: Columbia University Press, 1939. (ML 3102 P917)

14. Pratt, W. S.   The Music of the Pilgrims; a description of the
        Psalm Book brought to Plymouth in 1620. (Ainsworth Psalter) Boston:
        Oliver Ditson Co., 1921. (M 2116 P61)

15. Ravenscroft, T.   The Whole Booke of Psalms. London, 1633.
        (Vault M 2136 R254)

16. Sternhold, T. (Sterneholde) One and Fiftie Psalmes. Printed for the Eng-
        lish congregation at Geneva by John Crespin, 1556. Facsimile edition.
        (M 2.8 S839p)

17. Sternhold. T. (Sterneholde) The Whole Booke of Psalmes; Collected into
        English Meeter by Thomas Sternehold, John Hopkins and others. London:
        Printed for the Company of Stationers, 1624. (Vault M 1490 S839. Bound
        at the end of the book)

18. Sternhold, T.   The Whole Book of Psalms Collected into English
        Metre. London: Printed by J. Roberts of the Company of Stationers,
        1754. (M 2136 B812. Bound after Tate and Brady, M 19)

19. Tate, N., and N. Brady. The Psalms of David, a New Version of, Fitted to
        the Tunes Used in Churches. London: M. Jenour, for the Company of
        Stationers, 1718. (M 2136 B812) Also contains A Supplement to the New
        Version of Psalms by Dr. Brady and Mr. Tate. London: Eliz. Nutt, 1717.
        (Music)

20. Terry, R. R.   The Scottish Psalter of 1635. New York: H. W. Gray,
        1935. (M 2.3 S42T32) The Psalmes of David in Prose and Meeter With
        their whole Tunes in foure or more parts. Printed at Edinburgh by the
        Heiress of Andrew Hart, 1635. Facsimile following page 94.

21. Ye Olde New England Psalm Tunes (1620-1820) (YONE), ed. W. A. Fisher.
        Boston: Oliver Ditson Co., 1930. (M 2116 F537)

Records

TITLE	Recording	ESM No.
1. Confess Jehovah (Pilgrim Psalm, Ainsworth Psalter)	Bost ES-1	A 533
2. Early American Psalmody (Bay Psalm Book); Old Hundred, Windsor, Ten Commandments, Hallelujah, London, York, Pater Noster, Old 113th	New Rec 2007	LP 498 LP 917
3. Rosa (Early New Amsterdam Dutch)	Bost ES-1	A 533
4. Who is the Man? (Pilgrim Psalm, Ainsworth Psalter)	Bost ES-1	A 533
5. Music of the Pilgrims a. Nine Psalms from the Ainsworth Psalter. Psalms 3, 15, 21, 23, 24, 34, 100, 108, 136 b. Excerpts from Governor Wm. Bradford's "Of Plimoth Plantation"	HSL 2068	LP 1234

6 Iehovah he doth doe,
 what him doth pleafe:
in heav'ns and earth: in feas, and in
 all deep-places.

7 He caufeth vapours, from
the earths end, to mount-hye:
makes lightnings with the rayn:
out of his trefurye,
 the wind he brings.

8 Who fmote Ægypt,
from man to beaft,
 in their firftlings.

9 Both fignes and wonders-*ftrange*,
Ægypt in mdds of thee;
on Phar'oh and on all
his fervants, fend did hee.

10 Who fmote many-
great nations; and kylled Kings
 that were mighty.

11 Sihon th'Amorites King;
and Ogh king of Bafan:
and Can'ans kingdoms all.

12 And for poffeffion
 their land he gave:
to his folk Ifr'el, in poffeffion to have.

13 Iehovah, thy name *is*
unto eternitie:
Iehovah, unto age
and age, thy memorie.

14 For his people
judge; and repent, for his fervants,
Iehovah will.

15 The greevous-idols of
the heathen-nations,
they filver *are* and gold:
mens handy actions.

16 A mouth they have
and doe not fpeak:
eyes have they, and
 doe not perceive.

17 They ears have and hear not:
breath in their mouth is none.

18 Like them their makers be:
that trufts in them, ech one.

19 O Ifr'els houfe
blefs ye the LORD:

bleff ye the LORD,
 ô A'rons houfe.

20 O blefs the LORD, ye houfe
of Levi: blefs the LORD,
ye that the LORD doe fear.

21 From Sion let the Lord
be bleffe-*alway*:
which dwelleth in Ierufalem;
Halelujah.

PSALME 136.

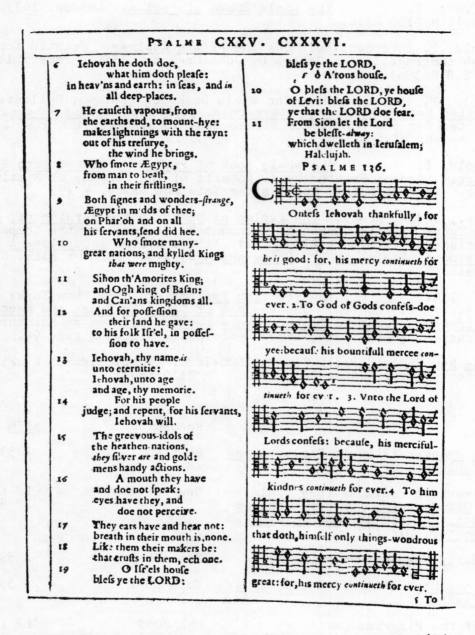

Ontefs Iehovah thankfully, for he is good: for, his mercy continueth for ever. 2. To God of Gods confefs-doe yee: becaufe his bountifull mercee continueth for ever. 3. Vnto the Lord of Lords confefs: becaufe, his merciful-kindnes continueth for ever. 4 To him that doth, himfelf only things-wondrous great: for, his mercy continueth for ever.

5 To

From The Psalmes in Metre by Henry Ainsworth, 1618

For he hath wrought throughout the
his wonders great and ſtrong.   (world,
2 With his right hand full worthily
he doth his foes deuoure:
And get himſelfe the victory,
with his owne hand and power.

3 The Lord doth make the people know
his ſauing health and might:
The Lord doth eke his iuſtice ſhew,
in all the peoples ſight.
4 His grace and truth to Iſrael,
in mind he doth record,
That all the earth hath ſeene right well,
the goodneſſe of the Lord.

5 Be glad in him with ioyfull voyce,
all people on the earth:
Giue thankes to God, ſing, and reioyce,
to him with ioy and mirth.
6 Vpon the Harpe vnto him ſing,
giue thankes to him with Pſalmes:
Reioyce before the Lord our King,
with Trumpets and with Shalmes.

7 Yea, let the Sea and all therein,
for ioy both rore and ſwell:
The earth likewiſe let it begin
with all that therein dwell.
8 And let the flouds reioyce their fills,
and clap their hands apace:
And eke the mountaines and the hils,
before the Lord his face.

9 For he ſhall come to iudge and try
the world and euerie wight:
And rule the people mightily,
with iuſtice and with might.

Dom.regnauit. Pſalm.XCix.I.H.

*He commendeth the power, equity, and excel-
lency of the Kingdome of God by Chriſt, ouer
the Iewes and Gentiles, prouoking him to
magnifie the ſame, and to feare the Lord, as
the ancient Fathers, Moſes, Aaron, and Samuel, who calling vpon God, were heard in
their prayers.*

*Sing this as
the 95.
Pſalme.*

THe Lord doth raigne, although at it
the people rage full ſore:
Yea he on Cherubins doth ſit,
though all the world doe roare.
2 The Lord that doth in Sion dwell,
is high and wondrous great:
Aboue all folke he doth excell,
and he aloft is ſet.

3 Let all men praiſe thy mighty Name,
for it is fearefull ſure:
And let them magnifie the ſame,
that holy is and pure.
4 The princely power of the King,
doth loue iudgement and right:

Thou rightly ruleſt euery thing,
in Iacob through thy might.

5 To praiſe the Lord our God deuiſe,
all honour to him doe:
His footſtoole worſhip him before,
for he is holy too.
6 Moſes, Aaron, and Samuel,
as prieſts on him did call:
When they did pray, he heard them well,
and gaue them anſwere all.

7 Within the cloud to them he ſpake,
then did they labour ſtill:
To keepe ſuch lawes as he did make,
and poynted them vntill.
8 O Lord our God, thou didſt them heare,
and anſweredſt them againe:
Thy mercy did on them appeare,
their deeds thou didſt maintaine.

9 O laud and praiſe our God and Lord,
within his holy hill:
For why, our God throughout the world,
is holy euer ſtill.

Iubilate Deo omnis.Pſal.C.I.H.

*He exhorteth all men to ſerue the Lord, who
hath made vs to enter into his Courts and Aſ-
ſembly, to praiſe his name.*

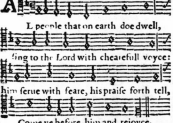

L people that on earth doe dwell,

ſing to the Lord with chearefull voyce:

him ſerue with feare, his praiſe forth tell,

Come ye before him and reioyce.
2 The Lord, ye know, is God indeed,
without our ayde he did vs make:
3 We are his flocke, he doth vs feede,
and for his ſheepe he doth vs take.

4 O enter then his gates with praiſe,
approch with ioy his Courts vnto:
Praiſe, laud, and bleſſe his name alwayes,
for it is ſeemely ſo to doe.

5 For why the Lord our God is good,
his mercy is for euer ſure:
His truth at all times firmely ſtood,
and ſhall from age to age endure.

Another of the ſame.

IN God the Lord be glad and light,
praiſe him throughout the earth:
Serue him and come before his ſight,
with ſinging and with mirth.

*Sing this as
the 67.
Pſalme.*

2 Know

25 Concerning thee shall be my prayse
in the great assembly:
before them that him reverence
performe my vowes will I.

26 The meek shall eat & be suffic'd:
Iehovah prayse shall they
that doe him seek: your heart shall live
unto perpetuall aye.

27 All ends of th'earth remember shall
and runne unto the Lord:
and thee all-heathen-families
to worship shall *accord.*

28 Because unto Iehovah doth
the kingdome appertaine
and he among the nations
is ruler Soveraigne.

29 Earths-far-ones, eat & worship shall:
all who to dust descend,
(though none can make alive his soule)
before his face shall bend.

30 With service a posterity
him shall attend upon;
to God it shall accounted bee
a generation.

31 Come shall they, & his righteousnes
by them declar'd shall bee,
unto a people yet unborne,
that done this thing hath hee.

23 *A Psalme of David.*

THe Lord to mee a shepheard is,
want therefore shall not I.

& Hec

2 Hee in the folds of tender-grasse,
doth cause mee downe to lie:
To waters calme me gently leads
Restore my soule doth hee:

3 he doth in paths of righteousnes:
for his names sake leade mee.

4 Yea though in valley of deaths shade
I walk, none ill I'le feare:
because thou art with mee, thy rod,
and staffe my comfort are.

5 For mee a table thou hast spread,
in presence of my foes:
thou dost annoynt my head with oyle,
my cup it over-flowes.

6 Goodnes & mercy surely shall
all my dayes follow mee:
and in the Lords house I shall dwell
so long as dayes shall bee.

Psalme 24
A psalme of David.

THe earth Iehovahs is,
and the fulnesse of it:
the habitable world, & they
that there upon doe sit.

2 Because upon the seas,
hee hath it firmly layd:
and it upon the water-floods
most sollidly hath stayd.

3 The mountaine of the Lord,
who shall thereto ascend?
and in his place of holynes,

E 5

Psalm 23 from the Bay Psalm Book, 1640
New York Public Library

"Low Dutch Tune" from the Bay Psalm Book, 1698
New York Public Library

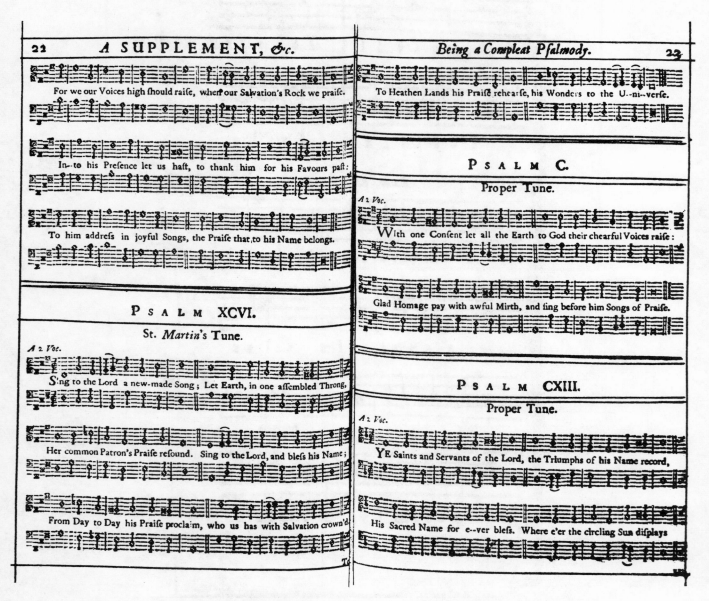

From A Supplement to the New Version of Psalms
by Dr. Brady and Mr. Tate, seventh edition, 1717

Frontispiece from <u>The</u> <u>Royal</u> <u>Melody</u> <u>Compleat</u> by William Tans'ur, 1764

From <u>The</u> <u>American</u> <u>Harmony</u> <u>or</u> <u>Royal</u> <u>Melody</u> <u>Compleat</u> by William Tans'ur, 1773

MUSIC IN NEW ENGLAND (1720-1770)

Instruction Books on Singing
Singing Schools--Secular Music
Early Church Organs

I. Instruction Books on Singing (1712-1764)

   A. The decline of church music
      1. During the 17th century the ability of congregations to sing in church declined rapidly.
         a. The second and third generations of Puritans found little time to cultivate the arts, and professional musicians seemed to be unknown. By 1685, even the tunes in the Ainsworth Psalter were considered too difficult.
         b. There were no printed tunes in The Bay Psalm Book until 1698 and by that time very few could "read by note."
         c. Instruments were not used in church and the practice of "lining-out" resulted in learning by rote a very few tunes and these imperfectly. Even the precentors became confused in "lining-out" the tune. Deacon Sewall wrote in 1705 that he intended to "set Windsor and fell into High-Dutch" and then set another tune "much too high."
         d. No two congregations sang a tune in the same way and when they met together, chaos resulted.
         e. "Lining-out" of the text often caused levity among the congregation especially when lines such as the following were read and sung separately:
            "The Lord will come, and He will not
            Keep silent, but speak out."
   B. In the early 18th century some of the more progressive ministers, among them Cotton Mather, began to complain about the singing in the churches, and tracts appeared advocating "singing by note" instead of "by rote." These tracts were followed by instruction books, and singing schools were eventually established.
   C. John Tufts (1689-1752)
      1. Born in Medford, Massachusetts, graduated from Harvard College in 1708, became a minister in Newbury.
      2. Published the first book in the English colonies on Psalm singing (about 1712). Copies of this edition, however, are not known. The third edition (Boston, 1721) was entitled A Very Plain and Easy Introduction. . . . The fifth (1726), and later editions (eleven in all), were entitled An Introduction to the Singing of Psalm Tunes. . . .
         a. The early edition, a book of only twelve pages, contained 28 tunes set in three parts: cantus, medius and "base."
         b. The settings are in Fasola notation, derived from an old English solmization system. The syllables faw-sol-law were repeated (beginning with the tonic note) with mi used to complete the seven notes of the scale.
            1) Tufts substituted capital letters F-S-L and M for the syllables and placed them on a staff with the usual G-sol and F clefs. A letter without a dot (F) indicated a quarter note; with one dot (F.) a half note; with two dots (F..) a whole note. Bar-lines were used only at the ends of phrases.
      3. Music: M 4.
   D. Thomas Walter (1696-1725)
      1. Born in Roxbury, Massachusetts, graduated from Harvard College in 1713, became a minister in Roxbury.
      2. The Grounds and Rules of Musick Explained; or An Introduction to the Art of Singing by Note was first published in Boston in 1721. The book was very successful, and at least eight editions appeared by 1761. It was first printed by James Franklin, whose brother Benjamin worked

in the shop.
    a. The book included a Preface signed by Increase Mather and others.
       The music, in three parts, was printed in score in diamond-shaped
       notes with regular bar-lines.
  3. Music: YONE p. 4; M 5.
 E. William Tans'ur (Tansur) (1706?-1783)
  1. Born in Warwickshire, England. He was an itinerant music teacher and
    singing master, and his collections of music were important contribu-
    tions to singing in England and later in America.
  2. The Complete Melody or Harmony of Zion was first published in England
    in three volumes (1734) with music arranged in 2, 3, and 4 parts. It
    was republished in 1755 and later as The Royal Melody Compleat. Parts
    of it were published in Boston in 1767 and, under the title American
    Harmony, by Daniel Bayley in Newbury-Port, Massachusetts. Among the
    good tunes that Tans'ur introduced in America were Croft's "Hanover"
    (Hymnal no. 288) and "St. Anne" (Hymnal no. 289).
  3. Music : YONE p. 6; Hymnal no. 68; M 2; M 3.
 F. Josiah Flagg (1738-1794)
  1. Born in Woburn, Massachusetts. He organized a militia band and gave
    concerts in Boston (1769-1773); settled in Providence later and fought
    in the American Revolution.
  2. In 1771 he put on the following program of "vocal and instrumental
    musick accompanied by French horns, hautboys, etc. by the band of the
    64th Regiment."

Program

ACT I.	Overture Ptolomy	Handel
	Song 'From the East breaks the morn'	
	Concerto 1st	Stanley
	Symphony 3d	Bach
ACT II.	Overture 1st	Schwindl
	Duet to 'Turn fair Clora'	
	Organ concerto	
	Periodical Symphony	Stamitz
ACT III.	Overture 1st	Abel
	Duetto 'When Phoebus the tops of the hills'	
	Solo Violin	
	A new Hunting Song, set to music by	Mr. Morgan
	Periodical Symphony	Pasquale Ricci

  3. A Collection of the Best Psalm Tunes in 2, 3, and 4 parts to which
    are added some Hymns and Anthems (1764). Engraved in Boston by Paul
    Revere. Most of the music was from English sources with some
    American music. This collection introduced the anthem to New Eng-
    land.
  4. Flagg was one of the first native Americans to concern himself with
    secular music as well as sacred.
  5. Music: LEAM p. 32; YONE p. 5.

II. Singing-schools

  A. Opposition to singing by note instead of by rote began before the pub-
    lication of John Tufts' book. Singing-schools were established in in-
    creasing numbers, however, with teachers travelling from place to place
    giving instruction.
  B. People who had learned to sing by note frequently sat together in
    churches; these groups were sometimes given a special place in the
    gallery, and the church choir was established.
  1. Efforts to continue the practice of lining-out the hymns were made,

but finally they were allowed to be sung straight through with the help of the choir.

C. Singing-schools were organized in Charlestown, South Carolina, in 1730, New York in 1754, Philadelphia in 1757. Revisions of older books and many new ones were published, including the Hymns and Psalms of David Imitated of Dr. Isaac Watts (1674-1748), which were reprinted in Philadelphia by Benjamin Franklin as early as 1729 and went through many editions.
1. Examples of hymn texts by Watts: Hymnal nos. 289, 319, 542.

III. Secular Music

A. Secular amusements were not encouraged in New England, and dancing schools were prohibited until the early 18th century.
B. Instrumental music
1. Brass instruments and drums were used to summon people to church and to give an alarm. Jew's-harps were used for trade with the Indians. Viols, virginals and other instruments were owned by the settlers and used in their homes.
   a. The Puritans disapproved of the use of the organ in church as it was especially identified in their minds with "Popery." The first organ in a Boston church was not installed until 1713.
C. Concerts
1. The first concert in the Colonies was given "at Mr. Pelham's great Room" in Boston in 1731. The concert began at six o'clock, and tickets were five shillings each. The names of the performers and the music played were not printed, however. Advertisements in newspapers usually stated that the concert would consist of "Select Pieces by the Best Masters."
2. Charles Theodore Pachelbell, son of Johann Pachelbel (1653-1706), the teacher of J. S. Bach's brother, was in Boston in 1733 and organist for a year at Trinity Church, Newport, Rhose Island.
3. Concerts were given in Faneuil Hall by Mr. Pelham in the 1730's and in 1754 there was a concert hall at Hanover and Court Streets.
4. There was considerable opposition to the theatre by the Puritans, and protests by Increase Mather (1686) and Judge Sewall (1714) are recorded. About 1750, laws were passed prohibiting theatrical entertainments.

IV. Early Church Organs (B 2)

A. Between 1713 and 1800 there were about twenty organs placed in New England churches, mostly Episcopal.
B. The first reference to an organ in New England was in 1711 (the Gloria Dei church near Philadelphia had an organ in 1703). Thomas Brattle, treasurer of Harvard College, imported the organ, and at his death in 1713 it was willed to the Brattle Street Church. This church refused the organ, and it was accepted by the Episcopalians in Queen's Chapel (later King's Chapel). In 1756 it was sold to St. Paul's Church, Newburyport. In 1736 it was acquired by St. John's Church, Portsmouth, New Hampshire and is there at the present time.
1. The organ had one manual and five stops: Stopped Diapason 8', Fifteenth 2', Principal 4', Sesquialtera (3 ranks), Dulciana 8' (possibly added later).
C. Trinity Church, Newport, Rhode Island (1733)
1. An organ built by Richard Bridge in London was installed and opened by Carl Theodore Pachelbell, son of the Nuremberg composer. The case is still used with the present organ.
D. Christ Church (Old North Church), Boston (1736)
1. Built by William Claggett, repaired in 1750, rebuilt in 1752. A new organ was installed in 1759. The case of the organ of 1750 was

retained and is in the church at the present time.
  E. St. Peter's Church, Salem (1743)
      1. Built by John Clark, traded in 1770 for an organ built by Thomas
         Johnston in 1754. This organ was sold to St. Michael's Church,
         Marblehead, in 1819.
  F. Christ Church, Cambridge (1764)
      1. One of the five organs in the Colonies built by the German-English
         builder, John Snetzler.
      2. The other Snetzler organs in New England are in the Congregational
         Church, South Dennis, Massachusetts; Historical Museum, Cooperstown,
         New York; Belle Skinner Collection, Holyoke, Massachusetts.
  G. First Congregational Church, Providence, Rhode Island (1770)
      1. This was the first organ to be installed in a church that was not
         Episcopal.

BIBLIOGRAPHY

Books

1. Brooks, H. M.   Olden Time Music. Boston: Ticknor and Co., 1888.
    (ML 200 B87)

2. Ellinwood, L.   The History of American Church Music. New York:
    Morehouse-Gorham Co., 1953. (ML 200 E46)

3. Fisher, W. A.   Notes on Music in Old Boston. Boston: Oliver Dit-
    son Co., 1918. (ML 200.8 B7F53)

4. Foote, H. W.   Musical Life in Boston in the 18th Century. Wor-
    cester, Mass.: American Antiquarian Society, 1940. (ML 200.8 B7F68)

5. Foote, H. W.   Three Centuries of American Hymnody. Cambridge,
    Mass.: Harvard University Press, 1940. (ML 3111 F6884)

6. Gilfillan, J. A.   Singing Schools in America. ESM Thesis, 1953.

7. Howard, J. T.   A Program Outline of American Music. New York:
    Thomas Y. Crowell, 1931. (MT 34 H849)

8. Johnson, D. L.   The Use of Instruments in the Worship Service in New
    England Churches from Colonial Days to about 1850. ESM Thesis, 1953.

9. Metcalf, F. J.   American Psalmody; or, Titles of books, containing
    tunes printed in America from 1721-1820. New York: C. F. Heartman,
    1917. (ML 120 V5M58)

10. Metcalf, F. J.   American Writers and Compilers of Sacred Music. New
    York, Cincinnati: The Abington Press, 1925. (ML 106 V5M58)

11. Metcalf, F. J.   Stories of Hymn Tunes. New York, Cincinnati: The
    Abington Press, 1928. (ML 3186 M588s)

12. Sonneck, O. G.   Early Concert Life in America (1731-1800). Leipzig:
    Breitkopf & Härtel, 1907. (ML 200.3 S69)

13. Stevenson, R. M.   Patterns of Protestant Church Music. Durham, N.C.:
    Duke University Press, 1953. (ML 3100 S948)

Periodicals

1. Cowell, W. K.   "The Organs of Trinity Church, Newport, R. I.,
    U.S.A.," The Organ XIV (1935), 245.

2. Freeman, A.   "John Snetzler and his Organs," The Organ XIV
      (1934-35), 34, 92, 163.

3. Redway, V. L.   "A New York Concert in 1736," MQ XXII (1936), 171.

4. Redway, V. L.   "Charles Theodore Pachelbell, musical emigrant,"
      JAMS V (1952), 32.

Music

1. Goldman, R. F.   Landmarks of Early American Music (1760-1800). New
      York: G. Schirmer, 1943. (LEAM)

2. Tans'ur, W.   The American Harmony or, Royal Melody Complete. (2
      vols.) Newbury-Port: D. Bayley, 1773. (M 2116 T168.8)

3. Tans'ur, W.   The Royal Melody Compleat; or the New Harmony of
      Sion. London: Brown, 1764. (M 2138 T16)

4. Tufts, J.   An Introduction to the Singing of Psalm Tunes.
      Eighth edition. Boston: printed for Gerrish, 1731. (M 2116 P974B)
      (Bound with Bay Psalm Book). Facsimile reprint from the fifth edition.
      Philadelphia: Musical Americana, 1954.

5. Walter, T.   The Grounds and Rules of Musick Explained; or, An
      Introduction to the Art of Singing by Note. Boston: Thomas Johnston,
      1760. (M 2116 W234)

Record

Title	Recording	ESM No.
Ballads in Colonial America	New Rec 2005	LP 494

a. King Henry V's Conquest of France (Traditional)
b. The Lamentable Complaint of Queen Mary
   (1680)
c. The Duchess of Suffolk's Calamity (1680)
d. Song of Six Queens Married to Henry VIII
   (1680)
e. A Voyage to Virginia (17th century)
f. The Mournful Lamentation for the Sad and
   Deplorable Death of Mr. Old Tenor (1750)

OUTLINE III

MUSIC SOUTH OF NEW ENGLAND (1700-1776)

Pennsylvania--The South--New York

I. Pennsylvania

A. Many religious groups from Central Europe settled near Philadelphia in the late 17th and 18th centuries.
   1. The Mennonites (1683) and Dunkards (German Baptists, 1719) believed in only the simplest church music. The Quakers were actively opposed to any music.
   2. The German Pietists (Mystics), however, under the leadership of Johannes Kelpius (1694) cultivated both vocal and instrumental church music.
   3. The Swedish church, Gloria Dei, was built in 1700, and an organ built by the Swedish maker, Hesselius, was installed in 1703.
      a. An account of an ordination service, with music provided by Kelpius, describes the use of the organ with the viol, haut-boy, trumpets, and kettledrums.
   4. Organs built by German builders were installed in Trinity Lutheran Church, Lancaster, Christ Church, the first Episcopal Church in Philadelphia (1728), and St. Paul's Church, Philadelphia (1763), and others.
B. Secular music in Philadelphia
   1. Music was first printed in 1729 by the Franklin Press. Lyon's Urania was published in 1762 and Francis Hopkinson's Collection of Psalm Tunes in 1763.
   2. Dramatic performances, consisting of plays, farces, and ballad operas took place as early as 1749.
   3. The first recorded public concert was given in 1757 under the direction of John Palma. James Bremner, organist of St. Peter's Church, organized concerts in 1763. "A Concert of Music, consisting of a variety of the most celebrated pieces now in taste, in which will be introduced the famous Armonica or Musical Glasses so much admired for the great Sweetness and Delicacy of its tone" was given in 1764.
   4. Music teaching began about 1730 with the announcement that Miss Ball, "lately arrived from London," taught "singing, playing on the spinet, dancing, and all sorts of needle work." In 1750 a music teacher announced that he taught "the Violin, Haut-boy, German flute, Common flute, and Dulcimer, by note."
   5. Benjamin Franklin (1706-1790) was interested in music, particularly from the philosophical and scientific viewpoint.
      a. He improved the Armonica (musical glasses) which became very popular between 1760-1800. The tone was produced by rubbing the glasses with moistened fingers.
      b. He is said to have been the composer of a quartet for open strings (M 3).
C. Ephrata Cloister
   1. Conrad Beissel (1690-1768) was born in the Palatinate, migrated to Germantown in 1720 and in 1735 established a community at Ephrata (Ephrata Cloister) near Philadelphia.
   2. Ephrata flourished as a religious and artistic center until the end of the 18th century, and hymns and chorals in as many as seven parts were sung.
   3. Beissel had very little musical training, but he composed a large number of hymn tunes which he set to his own texts and harmonized them according to his own theories.
      a. His hymn texts were printed in the Ephrata hymnal, the Turtel-Taube (Turtle Dove, 1747), and later editions had spaces to write in the music by hand.
      b. Beissel had many original theories regarding diets for singers. Among unsuitable foods were eggs, "which arouse numerous capricious cravings."

13

        c. Benjamin Franklin (1706-1790) published an Ephrata hymn collection in 1730.

    4. Music: M 1; B 9.

D. Bethlehem

    1. In the early 18th century Bohemian Brethren (Moravians), mostly German, colonized America, settling first in Georgia (1735), then moving to Nazareth (1740). Other colonists came from Europe to Bethlehem (1741), and congregations were established at Lititz, Lancaster, York, and later at Winston Salem, North Carolina.

        a. The Moravians were members of the Unitas Fratrum or "Unity of Brethren." This group of German Pietists was founded by the followers of John Huss about 1450, and became the first independent Protestant Church.

    2. The Moravians were intensely musical and organized a Collegium Musicum in 1744. This group performed orchestral, choral and chamber music by J. C. Bach, Johann Stamitz, Abel, Haydn, Boccherini, Handel, Graun, and Mozart, as well as that of their own composers. The organ, with string and wind instruments, was used in church services, and hymn singing was an important religious and social activity.

        a. An organ, built by the Swedish builder, Hesselius, was installed by Johann Clemm in the Moravian Church in 1746. Clemm and Tanneberger built organs in Bethlehem and Nazareth.

    3. Among the Moravia composers were Jeremiah Dencke (1725-1795), who came to America in 1761; John Antes (1740-1811), born in Pennsylvania; Johann Friedrich Peter (1746-1813).

    4. Johann Friedrich Peter, born in Holland, was the most outstanding of the Moravian composers. He came to Bethlehem in 1770, and then worked in Nazareth, Lititz, and Salem, North Carolina, returning to Bethlehem in 1793.

        a. His compositions include at least 50 anthems for voices and instruments. The early works use only strings and organ for the accompaniment, but later works (after 1793) require as many as ten wind instruments (flutes, clarinets, bassoons, trumpets, horns).

        b. The Six Quintets for two violins, two violas and violoncello (1789), written at Salem, are the first known examples of chamber music composed in the United States.

    5. Music: M 2; M 3; M 5; M 6; M 7-15.

II. The South

A. Charleston, South Carolina

    1. In 1670 the English established a colony at Port Royal, South Carolina and about 1680 built a church in Charleston. The French Huguenots had also settled in South Carolina and had a church in Charleston in 1681. Foreign musicians, particularly English, dominated the musical life and a singing school was founded in 1730.

    2. In 1732 the second recorded public concert in America took place. This concert was for the benefit of "Mr. Salter," and in 1737 a benefit concert was given for Charles Theodore Pachelbell, who lived in Charleston from that time until his death in 1750.

        a. The use of the term "benefit" in advertisements indicated that the concert was to be given entirely by professional musicians.

        b. The latest music from Paris (Gossec, Gretry) and London (Stanley, Handel) was being performed, and by the end of the century music by Stamitz, Martini, Haydn, Pleyel, Corelli and Mozart appeared on programs.

    3. An organ was installed in St. Philip's Church in 1728 and Pachelbell was organist from 1738 until his death in 1750.

    4. Mr. Thomas Pike announced in 1765 a "Concert of Vocal and Instrumental Musick performed by Gentlemen of the place, for the entertainment of all lovers of harmony. Concerts on the French Horn and Bassoon by Mr. Pike." Following is the program:

Program

Act I
French Horn Concerts
2d Concerts of Stanley
Solo on the Violoncello
5th Concerts of Stanley
Bassoon Concerts
Song
Overture in Scipio

Act II
French Horn Concerts
Concerts on the Harpsichord
Trio
Bassoon Concerts
Song
French Horn Concerts of Hasse

5. Music teachers prospered and lessons were given on the harpsichord, violin, violoncello, guitar, and flute. Most of the teachers were from England and included both men and women.
6. Ballad opera ("Flora, or Hob in the Well" by Cibber) was performed for the first time in 1735, and the St. Cecilia Society, the first musical society in America, was founded in 1762.

B. Williamsburg, Virginia
1. The British also dominated the life in Williamsburg, and the inhabitants "behaved themselves exactly as the Gentry in London."
2. Thomas Jefferson wrote in his Memoirs of the evenings of "musical diversion" at the Governor's Palace when he was a young law student at the College of William and Mary in 1765.
3. The Williamsburg playhouse was opened in 1732, and travelling companies performed contemporary operas not long after they appeared in London.
   a. "Love in a Village" by Thomas Arne, "The Clandestine Marriage," and "The Padlock" were performed in 1765.

III. New York
   A. The first public concert, for the "benefit of Mr. Pachebel," was given in 1736 and frequent concerts took place from that time on. A singing school was founded in 1754.
   1. The following program was announced by Mr. Caze in the New York Mercury, May 9, 1774:

1st Act.
A grand Orchestry's Symphonie
A French Ariette will be sung accompanied with the guitar and violin
Mr. Caze will play his own composed music, on the violin with Mr. Zedtwitz
A Concert on the Flute
A Sonada on the Spanish Guitar
The first Act to end with a March.

IId Act.
A Grand Orchestry's Symphonie
A French Ariette accompany'd with the Mandolin and Violin
A Solo on the Violin
A Duo on Mandoline and Violin
A Sonada of the Salterio; and d'Exaudet's Minuet with echos.
The Concert to finish with a March of the grand Orchestry.
After the Concert there will be a ball. . .

   B. William Tuckey (1708-1781) came from England in 1753 and settled in New York. He organized the music at Trinity Church, where an organ had been installed in 1741, and played an important part in the musical life of New York as organist, concert artist, conductor and composer. In 1770 he directed, for the first time in America, a performance of parts of Handel's Messiah (Overture and sixteen other pieces).
   C. Music: LEAM p. 25.

BIBLIOGRAPHY

Books

1. David, H. T. and A. T. Rau. <u>A Catalog of Music by American Moravians, 1742-1842</u>. Bethlehem: The Moravian Seminary and College for Women, 1938. (ML 120 U5R23)

2. Drummond, R. R.   <u>Early German Music in Philadelphia</u>. New York: Appleton and Company, 1910. (ML 200.8 P5D79)

3. Ellinwood, L.   <u>The History of American Church Music</u>. New York: Morehouse-Gorham Co., 1953. (ML 200 E46)

4. Gerson, R. A.   <u>Music in Philadelphia</u>. Philadelphia: Theodore Presser, 1940. (ML 200.8 P5G38)

5. Good, M. B.   <u>Some Musical Background of Pennsylvania</u>. Carrolltown, Pa.: Carrolltown News Press, 1932. (ML 200.7 P41G64)

6. Graf, H.   <u>The Opera and its Future in America</u>. New York: W.W. Norton & Co., 1941. (ML 1700 G736o)

7. Madeira, L. C.   <u>Annals of Music in Philadelphia and History of the Musical Fund Society</u>. Philadelphia: J. B. Lippincott Co., 1896. (ML 200.8 P5M18)

8. Messiter, A. H.   <u>A History of the Choir and Music of Trinity Church, New York</u>. New York: E. S. Gorham, 1906. (ML 200.8 N5T8)

9. Sachse, J. F.   <u>The Music of the Ephrata Cloister</u>. Lancaster: Printed by the Author, 1903. (ML 200.8 E63).

10. Scott, R.   <u>Music among the Moravians. Bethlehem, Pennsylvania</u>. ESM Thesis, 1938.

11. Sonneck, O. G.   <u>Early Concert Life in America (1731-1800)</u>. Leipzig: Breitkopf & Härtel, 1907. (ML 200.3 S69)

12. Sonneck, O. G.   <u>Early Opera in America</u>. New York: G. Schirmer, 1915. (ML 1711 S699e)

13. Vosburgh, T.   <u>The History of Vocal Music in Charleston, S. C.</u> ESM Thesis, 1937.

Periodicals

1. Hess, A. G.   "Observations on The Lamenting Voice of the Hidden Love," <u>JAMS</u> V (1952), 211.

2. Maurer, M.   "A Musical Family," <u>MQ</u> XXXIV (1948), 358.

3. Maurer, M   "The 'Professor of Musick' in Colonial America," <u>MQ</u> XXXVI (1950), 511.

4. Rau, A. G.   "John F. Peter," <u>MQ</u> XXIII (1937), 306.

5. Redway, V. L.   "James Parker and the Dutch Church," <u>MQ</u> XXIV (1938), 481.

6. Redway, V. L.   "A New York Concert in 1736," <u>MQ</u> XXII (1936), 170.

Music

1. Beissel, C.   Gott ein Herrscher. 7-part motet. New York: J.
   Fischer.

2. David, H. T., ed.   Ten Sacred Songs for soprano, strings and organ by J.
   Dencke, J. F. Peter, S. Peter, J. Herbst, G. G. Müller, J. Antes. Eng.
   text adapted by Carleton Sprague Smith. New York: The New York Public
   Library, 1947. (Music of the Moravians No. 1). Score only (M 1611 S123);
   Score and 1 copy each part (M 1611 S123DS)

3. Dickinson, C.   Early American Moravian Church Music. New York: H. W.
   Gray, 1954.

4. Franklin, B.   Quatuor pour trois Violons et Violoncelle. Trans-
   cription de Guillaume de Van. Paris: Odette Lieutier, 1946. (M 2.4 F831)

5. Herbst, J.   Das Volk, das im Finstern wandelt. Anthem for chorus,
   strings and organ. Score. Ed. Hans T. David. New York: The New York
   Public Library, 1938. (Music of the Moravians No. 10). (M 2042 H538V)

6. Hymnal and Liturgies for the Moravian Church (Unitas Fratrum). Bethlehem,
   Pa.: Provincial Synod, 1920. (M 2128 M831)

7. Peter, J. F.   Die mit Thränen säen. Anthem for chorus, flute, bas-
   soon, strings and organ. Score. Ed. Hans T. David. New York: The New
   York Public Library, 1939. (Music of the Moravians No. 2).
   (M 2042 P478D)

8. Peter, J. F.   Das Heiligthum ist aufgethan. Anthem for chorus, two
   flutes, clarinet, bassoon, strings and organ. Score. Ed. Hans T. David.
   New York: The New York Public Library, 1939. (Music of the Moravians No.
   7). (M 2042 P478H)

9. Peter, J. F.   Für mich, O Herr. Anthem for double chorus, strings,
   and organ. Score. Ed. Hans T. David. New York: The New York Public
   Library, 1938. (Music of the Moravians No. 11). (M 2042 W864F)

10. Peter, J. F.   Lasset uns rechtschaffen sein. Anthem for chorus,
    two flutes, bassoon, strings and organ. Score. Ed. Hans T. David. New
    York: The New York Public Library, 1938. (Music of the Moravians No. 3).
    (M 2042 P478La)

11. Peter, J. F.   Lobet den Herrn. Anthem for double chorus, orchestra,
    and organ. Score. Ed. Hans T. David. New York: The New York Public
    Library, 1938. (Music of the Moravians No. 6). (M 2042 P478Lo)

12. Peter, J. F.   Selig, wer in Jesu Wunden. Anthem for chorus,
    strings and organ. Ed. Hans T. David. New York: The New York Public
    Library, 1938. (Music of the Moravians No. 8). (M 2042 P478Se)

13. Peter, J. F.   Singet ihr Himmel. Anthem for chorus, orchestra and
    organ. Score. Ed. Hans T. David. New York: The New York Public Lib-
    rary, 1939. (Music of the Moravians No. 4). (M 2042 P478Si)

14. Peter, J. F.   Six Quintets for 2 violins, 2 violas and violoncello.
    Ed. Hans T. David. Score and parts bound separately. New York: The New
    York Public Library, 1939. (Music of the Moravians No. 9). (M 551 P478)

15. Peter, J. F.   Uns ist ein Kind geboren. Anthem for chorus, 2
    flutes, bassoon, 2 horns, strings and organ. Score. Ed. Hans T. David.

III-18   Music South of New England (1700-1776)

New York: The New York Public Library, 1939. (<u>Music</u> <u>of</u> <u>the</u> <u>Moravians</u> No. 5). (M 2042 P478U)

<u>Records</u>

<u>Composer</u> <u>and</u> <u>Title</u>	<u>Recording</u>	<u>ESM</u> <u>No.</u>
1. Peter, J. F.		
a. Quintet No. 1 (D)	New Rec 2013	LP 499
b. Quintet No. 2 (A)	New Rec 2014	LP 501
c. Quintet No. 3 (G)	New Rec 2015	LP 500
d. Quintet No. 4 (C)	New Rec 2015	LP 500
e. Quintet No. 5 (B-flat)	New Rec 2014	LP 501
f. Quintet No. 6 (E-flat)	New Rec 2013	LP 499
2. Antes, J.		
a. Go, Congregation, Go	Vic LM-57	LP 712
3. Ballads in Colonial America	New Rec 2005	LP 494

Interior of the Great Coliseum, built expressly for the Peace Jubilee of 1869. Looking from the Conductor's Stand toward the Chorus and Orchestra.

(See Outline XI)

Original of the seven-part motet
"Gott ein Herrscher aller Heiden" from the Turtle Taube
by Conrad Beissel, 1747

Modern edition of the seven-part motet
"Gott ein Herrscher aller Heiden" from the _Turtle Taube_
by Conrad Beissel, 1747

OUTLINE IV

THE FIRST AMERICAN COMPOSERS (1759-1800)

Francis Hopkinson--James Lyon--William Billings

I. Francis Hopkinson (1737-1791)

A. Born in Philadelphia, Hopkinson was a lawyer by profession. He was one of
the signers of the Declaration of Independence and held important government offices. He was a personal friend of George Washington and Thomas
Jefferson, and he was a cultivated amateur musician. He was probably a
harpsichord pupil of James Bremner of Philadelphia, whom he succeeded as
organist of Christ Church.

B. Compositions
   1. "My days have been so wondrous free" (1759) is said to be the first
      musical composition by a native American. The music was written in two
      parts in the style of English composers of the time, Thomas Arne (1710-
      1778), Shield (MWK p. 24), Storace and others.
      a. This song was included in a MS book of songs which was never printed.
         Other songs by Hopkinson in the collection were "The Garland," "Oh!
         Come to Mason Borough's Grove," "With Pleasure have I Passed My
         Days" and two religious compositions.
      b. Music: MWK p. 6; M 13; M 16.
   2. Seven Songs for the Harpsichord or Forte Piano (1788). These eight
      (the eighth was added after the title-page was engraved) songs were de-
      dicated to George Washington. In the dedication Hopkinson wrote:
      "However small the Reputation may be that I shall derive from this
      work, I cannot, I believe, be refused the Credit of being the first
      Native of the United States who has produced a Musical Composition."
      Washington replied in part: "I can neither sing one of the songs, nor
      raise a single note on any instrument to convince the unbelieving--
      But I have, however, one argument which will prevail with persons of
      true estate (at least in America)--I can tell them that it is the pro-
      duction of Mr. Hopkinson."
      a. As stated in an advertisement in the Federal Gazette, "these songs
         are composed in an easy, familiar style, intended for young
         practitioners on the harpsichord or forte piano."
   3. Music: MWK pp. 1, 20; LEAM p. 72; M 12 (facs. of Washington's letter);
      M 13-17.

II. James Lyon (1735-1794)

A. James Lyon, a Presbyterian minister, composer and editor of church music,
   was born in Newark, "East New Jersey." He graduated from New Jersey College (Princeton) in 1759; lived in Philadelphia until 1765 and then in
   Maine.
B. Urania or A Choice Collection of Psalm-Tunes, Anthems, and Hymns (1761).
   (M 20)
   1. The first American collection of Psalm-tunes which contained original
      compositions. The music is in two, three, and four parts. Instruc-
      tions on Psalm-singing were included, and the book was widely used.
   2. Six of Lyon's own compositions appear and there are a few attempts at
      "fuguing" and imitation, often in florid style.
      a. Psalm-settings include Psalms 8, 23, 95, and a two-part Hymn on the
         104th Psalm by Watts.
      b. Two of the twelve anthems in Urania are by Lyon: One based on
         Psalm 150 ("Let the shrill trumpets"), and one on two verses from
         Sternhold and Hopkins ("The Lord descended from above").
      c. The tune called "Whitefield's," which we know as "America," is set
         to the words "Come, Thou Almighty King" (M 20, 1. 190).
   3. Music: LEAM pp. 29, 30, 71; M 19; M 20.

III. William Billings (1746-1800)
    A. Boston tanner, patriot, and self-taught musician, Billings believed in
        American music for Americans. In spite of physical deformities, his
        energy and enthusiasm were extraordinary. The prejudice, at that time,
        against everything English made American music especially welcome, and
        he met with great success before and during the Revolutionary War. After
        the War, however, with the coming of foreign musicians, there was a
        strong reaction against the "crudities" of his music. He died in
        poverty and was buried in Boston Common.
        1. He made many contributions to musical life in America, stimulating
            the second revival of singing by founding singing societies and
            church choirs. His singing class in Stoughton became the Stoughton
            Musical Society in 1786. He advocated the use of a pitch-pipe and a
            bass viol to aid the singing and was opposed to the "lining-out" of
            tunes. Most of his music is of a religious nature.
    B. Musical style
        1. Billings wrote in The New England Psalm-Singer (1770) that he did
            not think himself "confined to any Rules for Composition laid down
            by any that went before me."
            a. He made use of the lively "fuguing" style, which at that time was
                revolutionary. The term "fuguing" was used in its older meaning
                of free polyphonic imitation and not in our sense of "fugue."
            b. Music direct and strongly rhythmic, with effective use of syncopa-
                tion.
            c. Melodies composed of simple intervals and modulation is rare.
               1) Principal melody generally in tenor part.
            d. Harmony square-cut, and triads are used on any degree of the
                scale, in any order, giving a strong primitive quality to much of
                his music. Inversions of chords are frequent, but the seventh
                chord is not used.
    C. Collections of Music
        1. The New England Psalm-Singer
            a. Engraved by Paul Revere. It included a chart showing the musical
                scale and solmization ("Gamut"), the terms and signs used in nota-
                tion ("Musical Characters"), and an "Explanation."
            b. Music: LEAM pp 33, 80, 85.
        2. The Singing Master's Assistant (1778)
            a. Called "Billings' Best." He answers critics of his first book
                (1770) who complained that the harmonies were too sweet, the
                tunes too simple. He composed his famous "Jargon," which had no
                concords, to show that he could write dissonant music.
            b. The collection contains 32 Hymns and 17 Anthems and the first ex-
                amples of fuguing tune, "music with more than twenty times the
                power of the old slow tunes."
            c. Tempo directions are given in various ways, based on the four
                "moods" of common time. Tempi were determined by counting the
                number of beats per second, relating the tempi to each other, and
                measuring the length of a pendulum that would swing the right
                speed. In The Continental Harmony (1794), tempos indicated as 80
                below are given as 75, but Billings probably preferred the faster
                tempo.

C		Adagio	quarter note - 60	3/2	half note - 60
¢		Largo	quarter note - 80	3/4	quarter note - 80
₵	2/2	Allegro	half note - 60	6/8	quarter note - 80
		2/4	quarter note -120	6/4	dotted half note - 80

            d. Chester (YONE p. 7; MWK p. 8; LEAM p. 88)
               1) Words and music by Billings, "Chester" became the song of the
                   Revolution. The tune has been the basis of compositions by
                   Luening and Schuman (M 18, M 21).
            e. Music: YONE pp. 7, 11, 12, 13.

3. <u>Music in Miniature</u> (1779)
4. <u>The Psalm-Singer's Amusement</u> (1781) (<u>M</u> 8)
    a. A later edition includes "A Gamut and Explanations of the Rules of Music" and "A Number of <u>plain</u>, <u>easy</u> and <u>useful TUNES</u> from the best Authors, ancient and modern, and well adapted to Schools, Churches and Families in the United States."
    b. <u>Concert of Modern Music</u> (<u>M</u> 7; <u>M</u> 8, p. 72)
      1) The text, probably by Billings, gives his ideas of composition. Said to be the "crowning achievement in his secular music."
    c. <u>Consonance</u> (<u>M</u> 3; <u>M</u> 8, p. 81)
      1) A song of praise of music, and one of Billings' few secular pieces, although he called it an anthem. Text by Dr. Byles (1706-1788), a descendant of Cotton Mather.
5. <u>The Suffolk Harmony</u> (1786)
    a. "The Lord is Risen Indeed" (<u>YONE</u> p. 18).
6. <u>The Continental Harmony</u> (1794) (<u>M</u> 4)
    a. Includes a chart of "Musical Characters," a series of eight short "Lessons" and a "Commentary by way of a Dialogue between Master and Scholar." Here Billings discusses again major and minor as "sharp" and "flat" keys and observes that the female sex prefers the "flat" (minor) keys.
    b. Music: <u>M</u> 5 (<u>M</u> 4, p. 117); <u>YONE</u> p. 30 (<u>M</u> 4, p. 129).

BIBLIOGRAPHY

Books

1. Ellinwood, L.   <u>The History of American Church Music</u>. New York: Morehouse-Gorham Co., 1953. (ML 200 E46)

2. Foote, H. W.   <u>Three Centuries of American Hymnody</u>. Cambridge, Mass.: Harvard University Press, 1940. (ML 3111 F6884)

3. Gilfillan, A.   <u>Singing Schools in America</u>. ESM Thesis, 1939.

4. Hastings, G. E.   <u>The Life and Works of Francis Hopkinson</u>. Chicago: The University of Chicago Press, 1926. (ML 410 H79H35)

5. Howard, J. T.   <u>The Music of George Washington's Time</u>. Washington: U. S. Government, 1931. (ML 200.3 U58) (<u>MWT</u>)

6. Sonneck, O. G.   <u>Francis Hopkinson and James Lyon</u>. Washington: H. L. McQueen, 1905. (ML 410 H79S69)

7. Strunk, O.   <u>Early Music Publishing in the U. S.</u> From Papers of the Bibliographical Society of America, Vol. 31, 1937, pt. 2. (ML 112 S927)

Periodicals

1. Goldberg, I.   "The First American Musician," <u>American Mercury</u> XIV, 67.

2. Lindstrom, C. E.   "William Billings and his Tunes," <u>MQ</u> XXV (1939), 479.

3. Pierce, E. H.   "On Some Old Bugle-Calls of the U.S. Navy," <u>MQ</u> XVIII (1932), 134.

4. Pierce, E. H.   "The Rise and Fall of the 'Fugue-Tune' in America," <u>MQ</u> XVI (1930), 214.

5. Winter, M. H.   "American Theatrical Dancing from 1750 to 1700,"
       MQ XXIV (1938), 58.

Music

1. Billings, W.   A Virgin Unspotted, ed. Dickinson. New York: Music
       Press, 1940. (M 2095 B598v)

2. Billings, W.   Be Glad Then America, ed. Dickinson. New York: Music
       Press, 1940. (M 2078 B598b)

3. Billings, W.   Consonance. New York: Music Press, 1947. (M 1584
       (M 1584 B598c)

4. Billings, W.   The Continental Harmony. Boston: T. Thomas and E.T.
       Andrews, 1794. (M 2116 B598)

5. Billings, W.   Hark! Hark! Hear You Not? ed. Dickinson. New York:
       Music Press, 1944.

6. Billings, W.   Jordan, ed. Lowens. New York: E. B. Marks, 1954.

7. Billings, W.   Modern Music. New York: Music Press, 1947.
       (M 1584 B598m)

8. Billings, W.   The Psalm-Singer's Amusement. Boston, 180-?.
       M 2116 B598P)

9. Billings, W.   The Shepherd's Carol. Boston: C. C. Birchard and Co.

10. Billings, W.   Three Fuguing Tunes, ed. Dickinson. (Creation; When
       Jesus Wept; Be Glad Then America). New York: Music Press, 1940.
       (M 2072.4 B598)

11. Fisher, W. A.   The Music that Washington Knew. Boston: Oliver Dit-
       son Co., 1931. (M 1629.5 F537) (MWK)

12. Hopkinson, F.   A Washington Garland, ed. Milligan. Boston: A. P.
       Schmidt Co., 1918. M 1630 H797wM)

13. Hopkinson, F.
       a. Beneath a Weeping Willow's Shade, arr. Daniel. New York: Carl
          Fischer, 1951. (M 1621 H797b)
       b. My Days have been so wondrous Free, arr. Daniel. New York: Carl
          Fischer, 1951. (M 1621 H797M)
       c. My Love is gone to Sea, arr. Daniel. New York: Carl Fischer, 1951.
          (M 1621 H797my)

14. Hopkinson, F.   The Psalms of David, transl. by Hopkinson. New York:
       James Parker, 1767. (M 2116 H797)

15. Hopkinson, F.   Seven Songs for the Harpsichord or Forte Piano (1788).
       Facsimile ed. Philadelphia: Musical Americana, 1954.

16. Hopkinson, F.   Six Songs by Francis Hopkinson, ed. Milligan. Boston:
       Schmidt Co., 1918. (M 1630 H797sM)

17. Howard, J. T.   Music Associated with the Period of the Formation of
       the Constitution and the Inauguration of George Washington. Washington,
       D.C.: U. S. Government, 1935. (M 1629 U58C75m)

18. Luening, O.   Prelude to a Hymn Tune by William Billings. New York:

Edition Musicus, 1943. (M 1004 L948P)

19. Lyon, J.   The Lord Descended from Above. New York: J. Fischer,
        1931.

20. Lyon, J.   Urania, or a Choice Collection of Psalm-tunes, An-
        thems and Hymns. Philadelphia: H. Dawkins, 1761. (M 2116 L991)

21. Schuman, W.   William Billings Overture. New York: G. Schirmer,
        1943.

22. Strunk, O. and C. Engel. Music from the Days of George Washington. Washing-
        ton, D.C.: U. S. Government, 1931.

Records

Composer and Title	Recording	ESM No.
1. Billings, William		
a. American Songs and Fuguing Tunes	Col M434	A 100
1) Be Glad Then America		
2) New Plymouth		
3) When Jesus Wept		
4) Creation		
5) Judea (A Virgin Unspotted)		
6) The Dying Christian's Last Farewell		
7) Chester		
b. A Virgin Unspotted	Bost ES-1	A 533
c. Chester (arr. for Orchestra)	Vic 4502	R 257
d. Chester (1770)	Bost ES-1	A 533
	Col 329	A 599
e. Lamentation over Boston	CHS 52	LP 485
f. David's Lamentation	CHS 52	LP 485
g. The Bird	Vic LM-57	LP 712
h. I Am the Rose of Sharon	Vic LM-57	LP 712
2. Cowell, Henry		
a. Hymn and Fuguing Tune No. 5	CHS 52	LP 485
3. Hopkinson, Francis		
a. My Days Have Been So Wondrous Free	Vic 10-300	R 1266
	Vic 4010	A 245
	Vic LM-57	LP 712
b. O'er the Hills Far Away	Vic LM-57	LP 712
c. Beneath a Weeping Willow's Shade	Vic LM-57	LP 712
d. My Love is Gone to Sea	Vic LM-57	LP 712
4. Luening, Otto		
a. Prelude on a Hymn Tune by William Billings	ARS 8	ELP 63
(Hymn to Music)		
5. Music of the American Revolution	WCFM LP-1	ELP 16
a. Washington March, Philip Phile		
b. Minuet, Pierre Dupont		
c. Brandywine Quickstep, Anonymous		
d. Beneath the Weeping Willow's Shade, Francis Hopkinson		
e. The Toast (to Washington), Francis Hopkinson		

Original MS of Hopkinson's "My days have been so wondrous free," 1759
The Library of Congress

From <u>Urania</u> by James Lyon, 1761

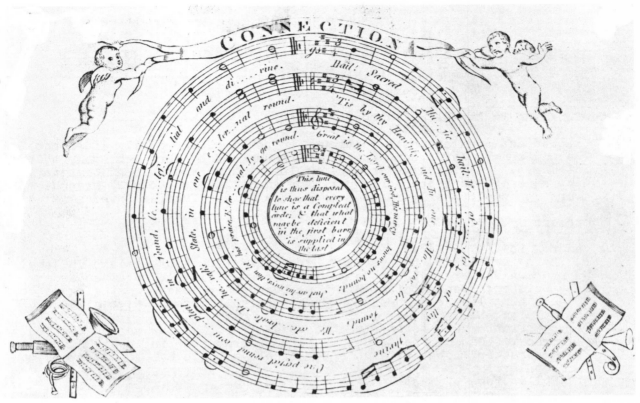

A round from the frontispiece of
The Continental Harmony by William Billings, 1794

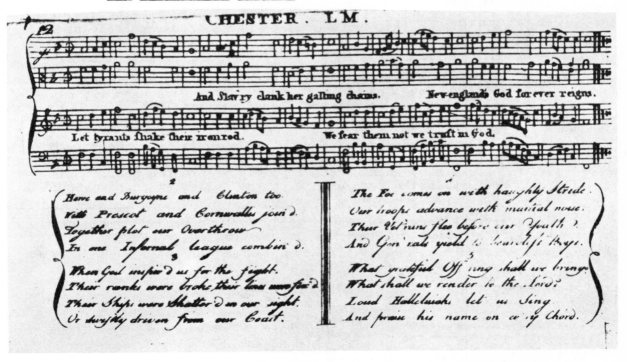

"Chester" from **The Singing Master's Assistant**
by William Billings, 1778

OUTLINE   V

MUSIC IN NEW ENGLAND (1770-1820)

New England in the Late Eighteenth Century
Composers--Secular Music

I. New England in the Late Eighteenth Century

   A. Sacred and secular music continued to develop, especially after the
       Revolutionary War. Concerts were frequent, and there were many teachers
       of music. Billings' music was popular with many of his contemporaries
       and some of his successors, but many Americans, especially preachers,
       were opposed to his frivolous and undignified "fuguing" pieces.

II. Composers

   A. Andrew Law (1748-1821)
       1. Born in Milford, Connecticut, graduated from Rhode Island College
           (Brown University) with a Master's degree (1778); ordained as a
           minister; spent most of his time composing, teaching singing-schools
           and compiling song books. He was actively opposed to the music of
           William Billings.
       2. Laws introduced to America the idea of setting the melody in the sop-
           rano instead of the tenor. He also introduced (in 1803) "shape" or
           "character" notes without staff lines, but his system never became
           popular.
       3. Collections of music
           a. A Select Number of Plain Tunes (1767)
           b. Select Harmony (1778)
           c. A Collection of the Best and Most Approved Hymn Tunes and Anthems
               (1779)
           d. The Art of Singing (in 3 parts, each separately paged, 1794)
           e. The Art of Singing, 2nd ed. (in 3 parts, consecutively paged,
               1800-01) (M 11)
           f. The Art of Singing, 4th ed., 1803. I. The Musical Primer, II. The
               Christian Harmony, III. The Musical Magazine (M 12)
               1) This fourth edition (1803) "with additions and improvements" was
                   "printed upon a new plan." Shape-notes were used without staff
                   lines, but the notes were placed relatively higher or lower.
               2) Major keys were called "sharp" keys and minor keys were called
                   "flat."
                   a) The "sharp" key of F required one flat and the "flat" key of
                       B required two sharps. The seventh degree in "flat" keys was
                       raised by an accidental placed before the note.
               3) Four syllables were used with the following shape notes:
                   "faw" □ , "sol" ○ , "law" ◁ , "mi" ◇ . "Mi" ◇ is the

                   seventh degree of the "sharp" keys and second degree of the
                   "flat" keys. A "movable do" system.
                   a) Major ("sharp") keys:

                       □   ○   ◁   □   ○   ◁   ◇   □
                       faw sol law faw sol law mi   faw
                       1   2   3   4   5   6   7   8

                   b) Minor ("flat") keys:

                       ◁   ◇   □   ○   ◁   □   ○   ◁
                       law mi   faw sol law faw sol law
                       1   2   3   4   5   6   7   8

4) Note values for "faw" ▢ (○ , △ , ◇ are the same):

▢| = ◯◯ ▢ = ○   ⊓ = ρ   ■ = ♩   ⊓ = ♪   ⊓ = ♪

5) The tempo marks were: "Very slow" with a beat of 1-1/2 seconds; "Slow" (1-1/4 sec.); Moderato (1 sec.); Cheerful (7/8 sec.); Lively (2/3 sec.); Quick (5/8 sec.); Very quick (1/2 sec.).
6) Common time (🅒 =4/2); Double common time (C =4/2)

   g. <u>Harmonic Companion</u> (1807)
     1) In his dedication to "ministers, singing masters, clerks and choristers," Law complains about the low state of church music and suggests that the ministers have the power to raise the standard.
     2) He uses his shape-note system with some improvements. A dot is added over or under the shape-notes for "faw," "sol," "law" in the upper part of the scale.
   h. <u>The Art of Playing the Organ</u> (1809)
     1) Not a method of playing, but the principles of his shape-note notation **as applied to the keyboard.**
  4. Music: <u>LEAM</u> pp. 43, 90; <u>YONE</u> p. 21; <u>M</u> 11-14

B. Oliver Holden (1765-1844)
  1. Born in Shirley, Massachusetts, Holden lived an active life as a carpenter, real estate operator, preacher, singing teacher, compiler and editor of song books, and composer of hymns and anthems. He settled in Charlestown in 1787.
  2. His musical training was limited, and he was a conservative composer; opposed to the lively "fuguing-tune" style of Billings.
  3. Collections of music
    a. <u>The American Harmony</u> (1792)
    b. <u>The Union Harmony</u> (1793)
    c. <u>The Charlestown Collection of Sacred Songs</u> (1803)
    d. <u>Sacred Dirges, Hymns and Anthems</u> (1800)
    e. <u>Worcester Collection of Sacred Harmony</u> (1803)
  4. Composed about 21 hymns; <u>Coronation</u> still used today (<u>Hymnal</u> no. 355).
  5. <u>The Massachusetts Compiler</u> (1795), edited by Holden included theoretical and practical explanations and a musical dictionary.
  6. Music: <u>YONE</u> p. 33; <u>LEAM</u> p. 100; <u>M</u> 5; <u>M</u> 15; <u>M</u> 19.

C. Samuel Holyoke (1762-1820)
  1. Born in Boxford, Massachusetts; composer and teacher of vocal and instrumental music; graduate of Harvard College (1789); organized Groton (later Lawrence) Academy.
  2. Opposed to use of brilliant "fuguing" style of Billings.
  3. Collections of music
    a. <u>Harmonia Americana</u> (1791)
    b. <u>The Columbian Repository of Sacred Harmony</u> (1802)
     1) Contains 734 tunes, many by Holyoke.
    c. <u>The Christian Harmonist</u> (1804)
    d. <u>The Instrumental Assistant</u> (1800?-1807)
  4. <u>Hark from the Tombs</u>, adapted from Watts, was set to music by Holyoke and performed in 1800 in memory of George Washington.
  5. Music: <u>LEAM</u> p. 59; <u>YONE</u> pp. 38, 40; <u>M</u> 6-8

D. Daniel Read (1757-1836)
  1. Born in Rehoboth, Massachusetts; compiler and publisher of song books and business man; lived in New Haven after the Revolution.
  2. Collections of music
    a. <u>The American Singing Book</u> (1785)
    b. <u>The Columbian Harmonist</u> (1793)
    c. <u>The New Haven Collection of Sacred Music</u> (1818)
  3. Music: <u>YONE</u> pp. 26, 27; <u>LEAM</u> p. 47; <u>M</u> 17-18

E. Timothy Swan (1758-1842)
  1. Born in Worcester, Massachusetts; only musical training was a few weeks in singing-school, but he composed some music of considerable

           originality.
      2. Collections of music
         a. The Songster's Assistant (c. 1800)
         b. The New England Harmony (1801)
      3. Music: YONE p. 37; LEAM pp. 49, 52
   F. Jacob Kimball, Jr. (1761-1826)
      1. Born in Topsfield, Massachusetts; graduated from Harvard in 1780;
         gave up profession of law to become a musician. His music is some-
         what in the style of Billings and a few of his tunes achieved
         popularity.
      2. Collections of music
         a. The Rural Harmony (1793)
         b. The Essex Harmony (1800)
           1) Both collections contain compositions by Kimball.
      3. Music: YONE pp. 28, 29, 30; LEAM pp. 54, 57; M 9-10
   G. Other native American composers of this period
      1. Supply Belcher (1751-1836) (LEAM p. 44; M 1)
      2. Daniel Belknap (1771-1815) (LEAM p. 62; M 2)
      3. Jacob French (1754-18--) (LEAM p. 94; M 3)
      4. Simeon Jocelin (Jocelyn) (1746-1823) (LEAM pp. 37, 39)
      5. Abraham Maxim (1773-1829) (YONE p. 47; M 16)
      6. Justin Morgan (1747-1798) (LEAM p. 41; YONE p. 23)
      7. Jezaniah Wood (1752-1804) (YONE p. 24)

III.   Secular Music

   A. Hans Gram, a Danish composer, composed the first orchestral score pub-
      lished in the United States, "The Death Song of an Indian Chief" (1791)
      (M 4). Gram was an editor, with Holyoke and Holden, of The Massachu-
      setts Compiler (M 15)
   B. William Selby (1738-1798), an English organist, teacher, editor, im-
      presario, and composer, was active in the concert life of Boston from
      1771 and organist at King's Chapel.
    1. During the Revolutionary War, when musical life was almost at a
       standstill, he made his living as a liquor dealer and grocer. In
       1782 he resumed his musical career.
      a. His concert programs included music by himself, Bach and Handel,
         pieces for band and chorus, and solos for voice and various in-
         struments, including organ pieces and a Concerto for Organ.
   C. Plays with incidental music were given in Boston; the anti-theatre law
      of 1750 was often avoided by using the terms "moral lecture" or "read-
      ings." By the end of the century the law was no longer enforced, and
      ballad-operas were regularly performed in the two Boston theatres.

BIBLIOGRAPHY

Books

1. Edwards, G. T.   Music and Musicians of Maine. Portland: The South-
    worth Press, 1928. (ML 200.7 M22E26)

2. Foote, H. W.   Musical Life in Boston in the 18th Century. Wor-
    cester, Mass.: American Antiquarian Society, 1940. (ML 200.8 B7F68)

3. Gilfillan, J. A.   Singing Schools in America. ESM Thesis, 1939.

4. Horn, D. D.   Shape-Note Hymnals and the Art Music of Early America.
    ESM Thesis, 1942.

5. Johnson, H. E.   Musical Interludes in Boston, 1795-1830. New York:
    Columbia University Press, 1943. (ML 200.8 B7J67)

7. Metcalf, F. J.   <u>American Writers and Compilers of Sacred Music</u>. New
     York: The Abingdon Press, 1925. (ML 102 U5M58)

<u>Periodical</u>

1. Maurer, M.   "The 'Professor of Musick' in Colonial America,"
     <u>MQ</u> XXXVI (1950), 511.

<u>Music</u>

1. Belcher, S.   <u>The Harmony of Maine</u>. Boston: I. Thomas and E. T.
     Andrews, 1794. (M 2116 B427)

2. Belknap, D.   <u>The Evangelical Harmony</u>. Boston: I. Thomas and E.
     Andrews, 1800. (M 2116 B432e)

3. French, J.   <u>Monmouth</u>, ed. Lowens. New York: E. B. Marks, 1954.

4. Gram, H.   <u>The Death Song of an Indian Chief</u>. New York: J. Fis-
     cher & Bro., 1931.

5. Holden, O.   <u>The Union Harmony</u>. Boston: I. Thomas and E. Andrews,
     1793.

6. Holyoke, S.   <u>The Columbian Repository of Sacred Harmony</u>. Exeter,
     N.H.: Ramlet, 1800. (M 2116 H761C)

7. Holyoke, S.   "Hark from the Tombs" (Manuscript), 1800.
     (M 2116 H761h)

8. Holyoke, S.   <u>Harmonia Americana</u>. Boston: I. Thomas and E. T. An-
     drews, 1791.

9. Kimball, J.   <u>The Essex Harmony</u>. Salem: T. B. Cushing & B. B. Mac-
     aulty, 1800. (M 2116 K47E)

10. Kimball, J.   <u>The Rural Harmony</u>. Boston: I. Thomas & E. T. Andrews,
     1793. (M 2116 K49)

11. Law, A.   <u>The Art of Singing; in Three Parts: to wit</u>, I. <u>The
     Musical Primer</u>, II. <u>The Ch(r)istian Harmony</u>, III. <u>The Musical Magazine</u>.
     Cheshire, Conn., 1800-01. Regular notation. (M 2116 L415)

12. Law, A.   <u>The Art of Singing; in Three Parts: Viz</u>. I. <u>Musical
     Primer</u>, II. <u>The Christian Harmony</u>, III. <u>The Musical Magazine</u>. Winsor,
     Vermont: N. Mower, 1803. Shape-note notation. (M 2116 L415a)

13. Law, A.   <u>The Christian Harmony</u>. Cheshire, Conn.: A. Law, 1794.
     (M 2116 L415C)

14. Law, A.   <u>Harmonic Companion</u>. Philadelphia: R. & Wm. Carr, 1807.
     (M 2116 L415H)

15. <u>Massachusetts Compiler</u>, The., ed. Holden, Holyoke, Gram. Boston: I. Thomas
     and E. T. Andrews, 1795. (M 2116 M281C)

16. Maxin, A.   <u>Sumner</u>, ed. Lowens. New York: E. B. Marks, 1954.

17. Read, D.   <u>The Columbian Harmonist</u>. New Haven, 1793. Fourth ed.,
     Boston: Manning and Loring, 1810. (M 2116 B282)

18. Read, D.   <u>Mortality, Norwalk</u>, ed. Lowens. New York: E. B. Marks,

1954.

19. <u>Worcester Collection of Sacred Harmony</u>, ed. Holden. Boston: I. Thomas and
    E. T. Andrews, 1803. (M 2116 W919.8)

<u>Records</u>

<u>Composer</u> <u>and</u> <u>Title</u>	<u>Recording</u>	<u>ESM No.</u>
1. Canning, T.		
a. Fantasy on a Hymn by Justin Morgan (1747- 1798) (Hymn in <u>LEAM</u> p. 41)	Mer MG-40001	ELP 62
2. Kimball, J.		
a. Bradford (1793)	Col M-329	A 599
3. Law, A.		
a. The American Hero (1775)	Col M-329	A 599
b. Bunker Hill	Vic LM-57	LP 712
4. Sumner, J.		
a. Ode on Science (1798)	Bost ES-I	A 533
	Col M-329	A 599

From <u>Harmonic</u> <u>Companion,</u> <u>and</u> <u>Guide</u> <u>to</u> <u>Social</u> <u>Worship</u>
by Andrew Law, 1807

Trinity.

Lively.

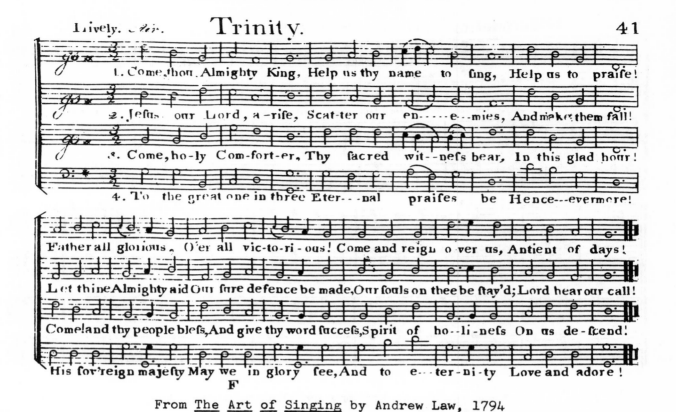

From The Art of Singing by Andrew Law, 1794

TRINITY. No. 128.

From The Art of Singing by Andrew Law, 1803

Coronation. C. M. Words by the Rev. Mr. Medley. **Original.**

All hail the power of Je-fus' name, Let angels proftrate fall, Bring forth the royal di-a-dem, And

crown him Lord of all, Bring forth the royal di-a-dem, and crown him Lord of all.

From The Union Harmony by Oliver Holden, 1793

98   *Marblehead.* C. M.

And fee how youthful

In-dul-gent God! with pity'ng eyes, The fons of men furvey.

And

And fee how youthful finners fport In

And fee how youthful finners fport, In a de-

fin-ners fport, And fee how youthful finners

fee how youthful finners fport, And fee how youthful, &c.

In a deftructive way.

a deftructive way, And fee how youthful finners fport,

ftructive way, And fee, &c.

From The Rural Harmony by Jacob Kimball, Jun. A.B., 1793

OUTLINE VI

FOREIGN MUSICIANS IN NEW YORK AND PHILADELPHIA (1780-1825)

The State of Music--Composers--National Airs

I. The State of Music

A. There was little musical activity in Philadelphia during the Revolution
    (1775-1783). However, the British, although in control of New York from
    1776-1783, patronized concerts and theatrical performances.

B. At the end of the Revolutionary War in 1783, foreign composers, perform-
    ers, and teachers from England, France, Germany, and Italy began to ar-
    rive in large numbers and soon took over the musical life.

    1. Their activity was centered chiefly in New York, Philadelphia,
        Charleston and Boston.

    2. The music of the first native American composers, Hopkinson, Lyon and
        Billings, ceased to appear on programs.

    3. The foreign musicians often appeared on the programs as composer, per-
        former and concert manager, but the music of Haydn, Mozart, Beethoven,
        Gossec, Stamitz, Pleyel, Gretry, J. C. Bach, Handel, and other well-
        known European masters was also played.

C. The Musical Fund Society of Philadelphia was organized January 7, 1820,
    for "the relief and support of decayed musicians and their families."
    Concerts and lectures were given to raise funds.

    1. Among musicians connected with the Society in its early days were
        Benjamin Carr, Raynor Taylor and Francis Hopkinson.

    2. The programs were often of the mixed variety, but such ambitious works
        as Haydn's Creation (1822), Beethoven's Mount of Olives, Handel's
        Messiah and the Dettingen Te Deum (1823, 1824) were performed.

    3. Ballad-operas continued to be performed, among them Storace's No Song
        No Supper, Shield's Poor Soldier and Bishop's Clari, the Maid of
        Milan. The latter includes the original version of "Home, Sweet
        Home." (M 3-5)

D. Subscription concerts were given in New York in 1782 by the British and
    were established after the war by William Brown. Theatrical entertain-
    ments were resumed in 1785 by the reorganized American Company.

    1. The following program, presented in New York, April 27, 1782 by the
        British, was announced:

THEATRE
(By Permission)

     This evening will be performed, a Concert of Vocal and Instrumental
Musick, for the benefit of two distressed Refugee Families;
     It is hoped the humanity of the respectable public will, on this laud-
able occasion, be particularly shewn, as they may depend upon every pains
being taken to render the evening's amusement agreeable.

Act I

Sinfonie of .. ..Toeschi
Quartetto of Davaux for violins
Song by Mrs. Hyde 'Soldiers tir'd of Wars alarms'
Violino Solo Concerto of.. .. ..Borchny
Quintetto of C. Bach for Flauto
Sinfonie of Stamitz.

Act II

Sinfonie of Haydn
Quartetto of Kammell, for violino
Song by Mrs. Hyde, 'The lark's shrill notes'

29

Hoboy Solo Concerto of C. Fischer
Sinfonie of .. ..Haydn

Act III

Sinfonie of .. .. Bach
Quartetto of Davaux, for violino
Song by Mrs. Hyde 'If 'tis joy to wound a lover'
Quartetto of Toeschi, for Flauto
Sinfonie of Mardino [Martini?]

Tickets to be had of the different printers, at Mr. Strachan's Coffee House, and Mr. James M'Ewer's No. 242 Queenstreet. Boxes 8 s. Pit 6 s. Gallery 4 s.

2. The following program was given in 1789 under the direction of Messrs. Reinagle and Capron:

Act 1st

Overture of .. .. Giordani
Song by .. .. Mrs. Sewell
Concerto Violoncello .. .. Mr. Capron
Overture of .. ..Guglielmi

Act 2nd

Overture of .. .. Stamitz
Song by .. .. Mrs. Sewell
Sonata Piano Forte.. .. ..Mr. Reinagle
Overture of .. ..Gossec

After the first act will be performed a Chorus to the words that were sung, as Gen. Washington passed the bridge at Trenton -- the Music now composed by Mr. Reinagle.

II. Composers

A.   Peter Albrecht van Hagen, Sr.
    1. Born in Holland. He came to Charlestown, South Carolina, in 1774. His son, Peter, Jr., was born there is 1781. Van Hagen, Sr. taught string and keyboard instruments and composition. He moved to New York in 1789 and made his debut there with his son, Peter, Jr., in the following program:

Act I

Symphony of .. ..Pleyel
Concerto on the Violin .. .. Mr. Van Hagen
Song .. ..Mr. Van Hagen, junior
                              (eight years of age)
Quartetto of   .. ..Pleyel
Concerto on the Tenor.. .. ..Mr. Van Hagen
Concerto on the Piano Forte.. Mr. Van Hagen, jun.

Act II

Concerto on the Violin .. ..   Mr. Van Hagen
Trio, Piano Forte
Song Duet.. .. .. .. Messrs. Frobel and Van Hagen
Solo upon iron nails, called Violin Harmonika
                              (never performed)
Symphony De Chasse, Finale   C. Stamitz

2. This musical family (Mrs. Van Hagen and her daughter were also musicians) moved to Boston in 1796. Van Hagen and his son opened a "Musical Magazine and Warrented Piano Forte Warehouse." He conducted the Haymarket Theatre orchestra and was organist at Stone Chapel. His compositions were principally arrangements of ballad operas.
3. Peter Van Hagen, Jr. (1781-1837) composed songs and some instrumental pieces.
   a. Music: PAC I, 11, 32; II, 21.

B. Alexander Reinagle (1756-1809)
1. Born in Portsmouth, England, of Austrian parents. He was a pupil of Raynor Taylor and a friend of C. P. E. Bach. He settled in Philadelphia in 1786 and was active there and in New York as a teacher, singer, pianist, conductor, composer and concert manager. He frequently appeared in concerts with Capron, Moller, and the Belgian violinist and composer, Joseph Gehot (b. 1756).
2. His compositions include: 6 Sonatas ... with Accompaniment for a Concerto for the Improved Pianoforte with Additional Keys (1794); Sonatas for Pianoforte (c. 1800); Songs.
   a. His music shows the influence of C. P. E. Bach and, to some extent, Haydn. His "Federal March" (1788) was played in a parade in Philadelphia on July 4 to celebrate the ratification of the Federal Constitution.
3. Music: LEAM p. 96; EAPM p. 1; PAC I, 19; PAC II, 25; MDGW pp. 22, 32; M 14-17

C. James Hewitt (1770-1827)
1. Born in Dartmoor, England; pupil of Viotti. He came to New York in 1792 and was active as a composer, publisher, violinist, organist and concert manager in New York, Philadelphia, and Boston. His son, John Hill Hewitt (1801-1890) became a well-known composer of ballads (EMCS pp. 28, 31, 34).
2. Music: PAC II, 17; MDGW pp. 2, 8; EAPM p. 26; M 7-8

D. Raynor Taylor (c. 1747-1825)
1. Born in England; chorister in Chapel Royal; organist in Chelmsford; music-director at Sadler's Wells Theatre in London. He came to America in 1792 and lived in Baltimore, Annapolis, Philadelphia (organist of St. Peter's Church).
2. Music: EAPM p. 20; PAC I, 22; PAC II, 10; M 20-31

E. Benjamin Carr (1769-1831)
1. Born in England; organist, pianist, ballad and opera singer, composer. He came to Philadelphia in 1793 and established the first American music store, "Carr's Musical Repository" (a branch in New York was sold to James Hewitt). He was the first publisher of American compositions and composed music for the play The Archers (1796). He was one of the founders of the Musical Fund Society.
2. Music: EAPM p. 28

F. Victor Pelissier (Pay-lis-ya')
1. Born in France, he came to America in 1792. He was a horn virtuoso and composer and lived in New York and Philadelphia. He played in a travelling opera orchestra (The Old American Company) and composed music for the play Edwin and Angelina (1796).
2. Music: EAPM p. 24; PAC I, 5; PAC II, 5

G. John Christopher Moller (d. 1803)
1. Probably came from Germany by way of England; arrived in New York in 1790. He was an organist, violist, harpsichordist and composer. In 1791-92 he went to Philadelphia and took part in the City Concerts, both as manager and performer, with Reinagle and Henri Capron, the French cellist and composer. He was an organist in Philadelphia and ran a music store and school with Capron. He succeeded Hewitt as manager of New York City Concerts with the Van Hagens.

2. Composed 6 Quartettos; 6 Sonatas for Forte Piano or Harpsichord;
    Variations for clavecin; pieces for Franklin's musical glasses.
3. Music: EAPM p. 33; MDGW p. 44 (Capron)

III.   National Airs

A. The first national airs, Yankee Doodle and Hail! Columbia, appeared
    in the second half of the 18th century and The Star-Spangled Banner
    and America in the early 19th century.
    1. Yankee Doodle
        a. The origin of the tune is unknown. It was referred to in 1767,
            was first printed in Glasgow in 1782, and in America in 1795.
        b. Many sets of verses were written to the tune, and it was used
            by the British to ridicule the Yankees who soon took it over as
            their own song with new verses. The best known verse, "Yankee
            Doodle came to town Riding on a pony, Stuck a feather in his
            cap, And called it macaroni," was known around 1764.
            1) The word "Doodle" may have been a corruption of "Do-little"
                and "macaroni" means a "dandy."
        c. Music: MWK p. 4
    2. Hail! Columbia
        a. The verses were composed in 1798 by Joseph Hopkinson, son of
            Francis, to stir up American spirit at the time when a war with
            France was being considered.
        b. The verses were set to the "President's March" written during
            Washington's administration by Philip Phile (d. 1793).
        c. Hail! Columbia was used as one of our patriotic anthems until
            the Spanish-American War, when the Star-Spangled Banner was
            used by Admiral Dewey as the official anthem for the Army and
            Navy.
        d. Music: MWK p. 16
    3. The Star-Spangled Banner
        a. The verses were written during the War of 1812 by Francis
            Scott Key as he watched the British bombard Fort McHenry in
            1814.
            1) The words were soon adapted to the popular English drinking
                song To Anacreon in Heaven, probably composed by John Staf-
                ford Smith (1750-1836).
        b. It was made the National Anthem by an Act of Congress on March
            31, 1931.
        c. Music: MWK p. 22; M 12; M 18; M 19
    4. America
        a. The words of "My Country 'Tis of Thee" were written in 1831 by
            Samuel Francis Smith (1808-1897) at the suggestion of Lowell
            Mason. It was adapted to the music of the British national
            anthem "God Save the King," written by the English composer
            Henry Carey (1685-1743).
        b. Music: MWK p. 14; M 2

BIBLIOGRAPHY

Books

1. Howard, J. T.   A Program Outline of American Music. New York:
    Thomas Y. Crowell Co., 1931. (MT 34 H849)

2. Jackson, G. S.   Early Songs of Uncle Sam.   Boston: Bruce Humphries,
    1933. (ML 3551 J121)

3. Johnson, H. E.   Musical Interludes in Boston, 1795-1830. New York:
    Columbia University Press, 1943.

4. Kobbe, G.   Famous American Songs. New York: Thomas Y. Crowell
        Co., 1906. (ML 3551 K75)

5. Muller, J.   The Star-Spangled Banner, 1814-1864. New York: A.
        Baker and Co., Inc., 1935. (ML 128 S79M95)

6. Sonneck, O. G.   A Bibliography of Early Secular American Music (18th
        century), revised by W. T. Upton. Washington: The Library of Congress,
        1945. (ML 120 U5S6.2)

7. Sonneck, O. G.   Early Opera in America. New York: G. Schirmer, 1915.
        (ML 1711 S699e)

8. Sonneck, O. G.   Report on "The Star-Spangled Banner," "Hail Columbia,"
        "America,""Yankee Doodle." Washington: Government Printing Office,
        1909. (ML 3561 S69)

Periodicals

1. Howard, J. T.   "The Hewitt Family in American Music," MQ XVII (1931),
        25.

2. Kidson, F.   "Some Guesses about Yankee Doodle," MQ III (1917), 98.

3. Krohn, E. C.   "Alexander Reinagle as Sonatist," MQ XVIII (1932),140.

4. La Laurencie, L.   "America in the French Music of the 17th and 18th
        Centuries," MQ VII (1921), 284.

5. Maginty, E. A.   "America, The Origin of its Melody," MQ XX (1934),259.

6. Norton, M. D. H.   "Haydn in America (before 1820)," MQ XVIII (1932),309.

7. Redway, V. L.   "The Carrs, American Music Publishers," MQ XVIII (1932)
        150.

8. Redway, V. L.   "Handel in Colonial and Post-Colonial America,"
        MQ XXI (1935), 190.

9. Winter, M. H.   "American Theatrical Dancing from 1750 to 1800,"
        MQ XXIV (1938), 58.

Music

1. Aitken, J.   A Compilation of the Litanies and Vespers Hymns and
        Anthems as they are Sung in the Catholic Church (1787). Facsimile ed.
        Philadelphia: Musical Americana, 1954.

2. America. Facsimile of original text and first printing. Privately printed,
        1931. (M 1630.A6 A512)

3. Bishop, Sir H.   Clari, or The Maid of Milan. Opera in Three Acts.
        Performed at the Theatre Royal Covent Garden, May 8, 1823. Original
        holograph score. (Vault)

4. Bishop, Sir H.   Clari, or The Maid of Milan. (The poetry by J. H.
        Payne) London: Goulding, D'Almaine, Potter & Co., 1823. Vocal score.
        (M 1503 B622C)

5. Bishop, Sir H.   "Home! Sweet Home" from Clari, the Maid of Milan.
        Composed and partly founded on a Sicilian Air. London: Goulding, D'Al-
        maine & Co., 182-? (M 1508 B622Ch)

6. Elson, L. C.   The National Music of America and its Sources. Boston:
        L. C. Page & Co., 1900. (ML 3551 E49)

7. Hewitt, J.   Six Easy Duets for 2 violins, or flute and violin.
        New York: J. Hewitt's Musical Repository. (M 287 H611)

8. Hewitt, J.   The Wounded Hussar, for voice and piano. Philadelphia:
        G. E. Blake. (M 1.A1 H611w)

9. Hopkinson, J.   Hail Columbia (1798). (M 2.8 H151)

10. Howard, J. T.   A Program of Early American Piano Music. (Music by
        Reinagle, Bremmer, Taylor, Palma, Pelissier, Hewitt, Carr, Moller) New
        York: J. Fischer and Bro., 1931. (M 21 H849) (EAPM)

11. Howard, J. T.   A Program of Early and Mid-nineteenth Century Songs.
        (Music by Horn, Knight, Russell, Baker, Clifton, Hewitt) New York: J.
        Fischer and Bro., 1931. (M 1629 H849) (EMCS)

12. Key, F. S.   The Star-Spangled Banner (facsimile). (M 2.8 K44)

13. Milligan, H. V.   Pioneer American Composers, 2 vols. Boston: Arthur P.
        Schmidt and Co., 1921. (M 1619 M65) (PAC)

14. Reinagle, A.   Chorus sung before Gen. Washington in 1789. Phila-
        delphia: H. Rice. (M 1659 W31R36)

15. Reinagle, A.   Claudine (In a Selection of the most admired Ballads)
        1801. (M 1507 S464)

16. Reinagle, J. (Brother of A. Reinagle). A Concise Introduction to the Art of
        Playing the Violoncello. London: Goulding, Phipps and D'Almaine,(1800?)
        (MT 302 R364)

17. Reinagle, A.   Cousin John, for voice and piano. Philadelphia:
        Blake's Musical Repository. (M 1.A1 R364c)

18. Smith, J. S.   The Star-Spangled Banner. Easy to sing version, ed.
        Martino. Boston: Eastern Music Co., 1941. (M 1630.S7 S652M)

19. Smith, J. S.   The Star-Spangled Banner. Arr. by Igor Strawinsky.
        New York: Mercury Music Corp., 1941. (M 1630.S7 S652S)

20. Taylor, R.   The American Tar, for voice and piano. Philadelphia:
        Carr's Repository, 1796. (M 1.A1 T245i)

21. Taylor, R.   Ching Chit Quaw, a favorite air. London: Printed for
        S. A. & P. Thompson (178-?) (M 1526 T245c)

22. Taylor, R.   En Verite, for voice and piano. London: Lambeth
        (179-?) (M 1526 T245e)

23. Taylor, R.   The Female Ballad Singer. Philadelphia: Carr and
        Schetky, c. 1800. (M 1.A; T245f)

24. Taylor, R.   Gay Strephon, for voice and piano. London: Lambeth
        (179-?) (M 1621 T245g)

25. Taylor, R.   Hark Hark the Joy Inspiring Horn. A hunting song for
        voice and piano. Philadelphia: G. Willig, c. 1805. (M 1.A1 T245h)

26. Taylor, R.   I'd Rather Be Hang'd, Than Be Married. London: Lam-

beth, 179-? (M 1621 T245i)

27. Taylor, R.   <u>Jockey and Jenny</u>, for voice and piano. Philadelphia:
     B. Carr, 179-? (M 1.Al T245j) (M 1621 T245j)

28. Taylor, R.   <u>The Silver Rain</u>. Glee for 3 women's voices and piano.
     Philadelphia: Carr & Schetky, 180-? (M 1.Al T245s)

29. Taylor, R.   <u>Sonata for the Piano Forte, with an Accompaniment for
     a Violin</u>. Philadelphia: Carr's Musical Repository, 179-? (M 1.Al
     T245so)

30. Taylor, R.   <u>Tally O! Hark! Away!</u> for voice and piano. Philadel-
     phia: G. E. Blake, 180-? (M 1.Al T245t)

31. Taylor, R.   '<u>Tis All a Joke</u>, for voice and piano. London: Lam-
     beth, 179-? (M 1621 T245ti)

Records

Composer and Title	Recording	ESM No.
1. Election Song. Jefferson and Liberty	Bost ES I	A 533
2. Franceschini, G. (fl. 1770-1800)		
a. Trio Sonata (2 violins, cello, continuo) (B^b)	New Rec 2006	LP 493
3. Gehot, J		
a. Quartetto in D	New Rec 2002	LP 496
4. de Leaumont, Chevalier		
a. Duo Concertante (1787)	New Rec 2004	LP 495
5. Moller, J. C.		
a. Quartetto in E-flat	New Rec 2002	LP 496
6. Reinagle, A.		
a. Piano Sonata in E	New Rec 2006	LP 493
	All 3024	E LP 69
7. Taylor, R.		
a. Sonata No. IV (D) (Cello and continuo)	New Rec 2004	LP 495
b. Sonata No. VI (C) (Cello and continuo)	New Rec 2004	LP 495

COUSIN JOHN

Sung with the greatest applause

by Mʳˢ WIGNELL

in the SAILOR'S DAUGHTER

Composed by A. REINAGLE.

Printed for the Author and Sold at Blake's Musical Repository Philadelphia.
_ price 25 cents _

A song by Alexander Reinagle

cousin cousin John.

2ᵈ VERSE.

Love has bow & arrows   gentle cousin   John   Should he aim a shaft at you,

Arrows mortal every one   gentle cousin John.

same shaft may wound me too. When that cruel deed is done, Then good evning, then good evning

cousin cousin John.

3ᵈ

Love has chains and fetters, gentle cousin John.

Hymen is a cruel knave,

For he puts those fetters on, gentle cousin John;

Makes his best of friends his slave.

Farewell love when that is done;

Then good night ah, then good night dear cousin, cousin John.

"Hail! Columbia" by Joseph Hopkinson, 1798

Brothers join'd peace and saf ty we shall find.

2

Immortal Patriots rife once more
Defend your rights — defend your fhore
    Let no rude foe with impious hand
    Let no rude foe with impious hand
Invade the fhrine where facred lies
Of toil and blood the well earnd prize
    While offering peace fincere and juft
    In heavn we place a manly truft
    That truth and juftice will prevail
    And every fcheme of bondage fail
        Firm — united &c

3

Sound found the trump of fame
Let Wafhingtons great name
    Ring thro the world with loud applaufe
    Ring thro the world with loud applaufe
Let every clime to Freedom dear
Liften with a joyful ear —
    With equal fkill with godlike powr
    He governs in the fearful hour
    Of horrid war or guides with cafe
    The happier times of honeft peace —
        Firm — united &c

4

Behold the Chief who now commands
Once more to ferve his Country ftands
    The rock on which the ftorm will beat
    The rock on which the ftorm will beat
But arm'd in virtue firm and true
His hopes are fix'd on heavn and you —
    When hope was finking in difmay
    When glooms obfcur'd Columbias day
    His fteady mind from changes free
    Refolved on Death or Liberty —
        Firm — united &c

For the FLUTE or VIOLIN

2ᵈ time Chorus

LOWELL MASON AND HIS CONTEMPORARIES

The Early Nineteenth Century
Lowell Mason--Contemporaries of Lowell Mason

I. The Early Nineteenth Century

    A. Foreign musicians still controlled American music, but many of the
    younger musicians became naturalized and were identified with American
    music during their entire artistic careers. These early musicians and
    their immediate predecessors, both foreign and native American, paved
    the way for Lowell Mason and other American composers.

       1. Gottlieb Graupner (1767-1836)
         a. This German oboist and composer played an important part in the
         early development of American orchestral music. He settled in
         Charleston in 1795 and in Boston in 1798, where he opened a music
         store and taught piano and orchestral instruments. He became an
         American citizen in 1808.
         b. He founded the Boston Philharmonic Society in 1810. This small
         orchestra of amateurs and professionals met for the playing of
         Haydn's symphonies and other works and eventually gave concerts
         (the last one in 1824).
         c. Graupner was also one of the organizers of a musical organization
         which became the Handel and Haydn Society (1815). This Society
         sang the works of Handel, Haydn and other "eminent composers,"
         raised the standard of choral singing, and helped in the formation
         of other choral societies.
       2. George K. Jackson (1745-1823)
         a. Came from London to Norfolk, Virginia, in 1796. Active in the
         South, New York, and in Boston, where he was the first organist of
         the Handel and Haydn Society.
         b. Published, through the Society, Lowell Mason's first Collection of
         Church Music (1822).
       3. Oliver Shaw (1779-1848)
         a. Born in Middleboro, Mass. Although blind, he became known as a
         singer, organist, composer and compiler of music, and teacher. One
         of his pupils was Lowell Mason.
         b. Music: YONE p. 48; M 39-44

II. Lowell Mason (1792-1872)

    A. Born January 8 in Medfield, Massachusetts. Mason began his career at
    the age of sixteen and became an outstanding organist, conductor, teach-
    er, composer, compiler of music collections, and organizer of singing-
    schools.
    B. Lowell Mason was a bank clerk in Savannah, Georgia (1812-1827) and be-
    came organist and choirmaster of the Presbyterian Church there, con-
    tinuing his studying, composing and compiling hymn tunes and anthems.
       1. His first book, published in 1822, was The Boston Handel and Haydn
         Society Collection of Church Music (M 24). This popular collection
         went through nineteen editions.
    C. In 1827 he moved to Boston, where he was well known through his Handel
    and Haydn Collection, and became choir director at Lyman Beecher's
    Bowdoin Square Church and president and conductor of the Handel and
    Haydn Society.
       1. He organized the first children's singing-school to train children to
         sing alto parts in church choirs, which rarely had altos.
       2. Collections of music for children's choirs soon began to appear. A-
         mong these were The Juvenile Psalmist, 1829, the first music book for
         Sunday schools, and The Juvenile Lyre, 1831, the first book of

secular school songs in America. (<u>M</u> 25, 27, 31, 35)
D. In 1832 he established the Boston Academy of Music with George J. Webb.
   1. He organized an annual teacher-training class at the Academy in 1834.
      This idea was soon extended throughout New England and the Middle
      Atlantic States by means of "conventions" and teachers and normal
      institutes. He travelled as far west as Rochester, N.Y., often meet-
      ing groups of several hundred singers and teachers. The festivals
      which developed from these conventions helped to spread his creed of
      "music for the masses."
   2. In his <u>Manual of the Boston Academy of Music</u> (M 29, p. 25) he stated:
      "It is not so much the object of education to store the mind with
      knowledge, as to discipline it. That person is not the best educated
      <u>who has learned the most</u>, but he who knows best how to learn."
   3. He had studied the Pestalozzi (1746-1827) system of teaching in 1829
      and used it extensively after that time. Pestalozzi had stressed
      the inductive method of instruction, "<u>building</u> up instead of <u>patch-
      ing</u> up."
E. Mason made a short visit to Europe in 1837. He studied musical in-
    struction in the schools, heard much music and met many musicians.
    Among the latter was Mendelssohn, who was rehearsing his oratorio
    <u>St. Paul</u> in London.
F. Mason worked toward the establishment of music teaching in the public
    schools and conducted classes for children (free if they came for one
    year) at the Hawes Grammar School (1837-38).
   1. In 1838 he was appointed superintendent of music in the Boston
      schools, a position he held until 1845.
G. In 1851 he went to Europe for the second time, and on his return in
    1853 settled in Orange, New Jersey, where he took an active part in
    community life.
   1. In London he gave lectures on "Music for the Church" and "Pesta-
      lozzianism," directed singing schools and music classes for
      children.
H. In 1853 he organized, with Hastings, Root and Bradbury, The New York
    Musical Normal Institute.
   1. The curriculum included theory, composition, instrumental and vocal
      training and choral practice. Sessions lasted for three months at
      a time.
I. In 1855 New York University awarded Mason the second honorary Doctor
    of Music degree to be conferred in this country.
J. Lowell Mason's elder sons, Daniel Gregory and Lowell Jr., established
    the publishing firm known as Mason Brothers. His son Henry was one of
    the founders of the Mason and Hamlin Co., makers of reed organs. They
    began the construction of pianos in 1882. Another son, William, be-
    came a famous piano pedagogue. Daniel Gregory Mason (1873-1953), son
    of Henry, was Lowell's grandson.
K. Mason led the reaction against the cheap "gospel song" type of hymn
    which had begun to appear after the "fuguing tunes" of Billings were
    discarded. His objectives were to improve the quality of church
    music, choir singing, and singing-school teaching.
   1. His teachers classes, conventions and normal institutes provided
      well-trained music teachers for over a quarter of a century.
L. Mason published well over a hundred collections, many in collabora-
    tion with his contemporaries, Hastings, Webb, Bradbury and Oliver, and
    several million copies were sold.
   1. The collections usually contained sacred and secular music and an in-
      troduction called "The Singing-School." This section included the
      elements of music, exercises, rounds, part-songs, hymns, and anthems.
      a. Airs or parts of compositions by well-known composers such as Han-
         del, Haydn, Mozart and Beethoven were often adapted and arranged
         with religious texts.
      b. The syllables do-re-mi were used in place of the old faw-sol-law-
         mi.

        c. The usual order of voices in open score was tenor, alto, treble, "base."

        d. Figured bass was used in many collections.

  M. Music

    1. Hymn tunes: <u>Olivet</u>, "My faith looks up to Thee" (<u>Hymnal</u> no. 449); <u>Bethany</u>, "Nearer, my God, to Thee" (<u>Hymnal</u> no. 465); <u>Hymnal</u> nos. 170, 254, 440, 495.

    2. Collections: <u>M</u> 22-36

III. Contemporaries of Lowell Mason

  A. Thomas Hastings (1784-1872)

    1. Born in Washington, Connecticut; author of many hymns and composed a large number of hymn tunes; editor of the <u>Western Recorder</u> of Utica from 1823 until 1832, when he moved to New York.

    2. He published about 50 collections, some in collaboration with Lowell Mason, William Bradbury and others. His <u>Musica Sacra</u> (M 17) was compiled with S. Warriner.

    3. Music

        a. Hymn tunes: "Rock of Ages" (<u>Hymnal</u> no. 471); "From every stormy wind" (<u>Hymnal</u> no. 421).

        b. Collections: <u>M</u> 16-20

  B. George James Webb (1803-1887)

    1. Born near Salisbury, England; came to Boston in 1830. He was associated with Mason in the organization of the Boston Academy of Music and played an important part in the musical life of Boston as an organist (Old South Church) and conductor. He followed Mason to Orange, New Jersey, and also taught in New York and held summer Normal Schools in Binghamton, New York and other places, frequently with Lowell Mason.

    2. His tune <u>Webb</u> was published in Mason's <u>Spiritual Songs</u> to a text by Samuel Francis Smith. Webb was editor of The Musical Library which included all types of vocal music and also dance music with directions for its performance.

    3. Music

        a. Hymn tune: "Stand up, stand up for Jesus" (<u>Hymnal</u> no. 562; also no. 264)

        b. Collections: <u>M</u> 45, 46

  C. William B. Bradbury (1816-1868)

    1. Born in Maine; attended the Boston Academy of Music of Mason and Webb; sang in Mason's choir at the Bowdoin Street Church and for a short time was organist there, performing "the double duty of pressing the keys to make the music, and pulling them up again to stop the sound;" taught piano and singing-schools in Boston and Maine and later in New York.

    2. He held his first musical convention in New Jersey and later joined forces with Mason, Hastings, and George F. Root. In 1854 he began the manufacture of pianos with his brother.

    3. Music

        a. Hymn tunes: "Just as I am" (<u>Hymnal</u> no 409); "He leadeth me" (<u>Hymnal</u> no 426)

        b. Collections: <u>M</u> 3-15

  D. Henry K. Oliver (1800-1885)

    1. Born in Beverly, Massachusetts; studied at Boston Latin School, Phillips Andover Academy, Harvard and Dartmouth (Mus.Doc., 1883). Leader in civic affairs, musician and teacher.

    2. Music: Hymn tune: <u>Federal Street</u> (<u>Hymnal</u> no. 423); originally written for another text; tune named for the Boston street where Oliver's boyhood church once stood.

  E. Benjamin F. Baker (1811-1889)

    1. Succeeded Lowell Mason as the teacher in the Boston Schools;

church-singer and director in Salem, Portland and Boston; vice-president of Handel and Haydn Society. Founded his own music school where he acted as director and singing teacher for seventeen years.
2. He collaborated with other musicians in compiling many song books which also included music by Handel, Haydn, Beethoven and others.
3. Music: M 1; M 2
F. Isaac B. Woodbury (1819-1858)
   1. Educated in Boston; studied in London and Paris in 1838; organized and directed The New Hampshire and Vermont Musical Association; in 1851 editor of the New Musical Review in New York (1851); director of music at the Rutgers Street Church; made a second trip to Europe in 1852.
   2. Compositions written for church, sabbath schools, singing-schools and the family circle. The Day Spring, published after his death, was widely used in singing-schools.
   3. Music
      a. The hymn tune Creation (Hymnal no. 309) was arranged from Haydn's "Creation."
      b. Collections: M 47-51

BIBLIOGRAPHY

Books

1. Birge, E. B.   The History of Public School Music in the U. S. Philadelphia: Oliver Ditson Co., 1937. (ML 200 B618.2)

2. Ewen, D.   Music Comes to America. New York: Crowell & Co., 1942. (ML 200 E94)

3. Foote, H. W.   Musical Life in Boston in the 18th Century. Worcester, Mass.: American Antiquarian Society, 1940. (ML 200.8 B7F68)

4. Gray, A.   Lowell Mason's Contribution to America. ESM Thesis, 1941.

5. Johnson, H. E.   Musical Interludes in Boston, 1795-1830. New York: Columbia University Press, 1943. (ML 200.8 B7J67)

6. Mason, H. L.   Hymn-Tunes of Lowell Mason, A Bibliography. Cambridge, Mass.: The University Press, 1944. (ML 134 M399h)

7. Mason, L.   Musical Letters from Abroad. New York: Mason Bros., 1854. (ML 410 M3992m)

8. Rich, A. L.   Lowell Mason: The Father of Singing Among the Children. Chapel Hill: The University of North Carolina Press, 1946. (Bibliography) (ML 410 M3992R49)

9. Scanlon, M. B.   Dr. Lowell Mason in Music Education. ESM Thesis, 1940. (Bibliography)

10. Sonneck, O. G.   Early Concert Life in America. Leipzig: Breitkopf & Härtel, 1907. (ML 200.3 S69)

Periodicals

1. Flueckiger, S. L.   "Why Lowell Mason left the Boston School," Music Educators Journal (Feb., 1936), 20.

2. Garbett, A. S.   "America's First Great Musical Pioneer," Etude (May,

3. Mason, D. G.   "A Glimpse of Lowell Mason," New Music Review (Jan.,
         1927), 49.

4. Rich, A. L.   "Lowell Mason, Modern Music Teacher," Music Educators
         Journal (Jan., 1942), 22.

5. Sabin, R.   "Early American Composers and Critics," MQ XXIV (1938),
         210.

6. Scanlon, M. B.   "Lowell Mason's Philosophy of Music Education," Music
         Educators Journal (Jan., 1942), 24.

7. Scanlon, M. B.   "Pioneer Music Maker," Music Educators Journal (Nov.-
         Dec., 1941), 18.

8. Sunderman, L. F.   "Lowell Mason, Father of American Music Education,"
         Journal of Musicology (Nov., 1944), 6.

Music

1. Baker, B. F.   Baker's Church Music. Collection of hymn tunes,
         chants, sentences and anthems. Boston: J. P. Jewett & Co., 1855.
         (M 2121 B167)

2. Baker, B. F.   The Choral; A collection of church music adapted to
         the worship of all denominations. By B. F. Baker and I. B. Woodbury.
         Boston: Otis, Broaders & Co., 1847. (M 2121 B167c)

3. Bradbury, W. B.   The Alpine Glee Singer; A complete collection of
         secular and social music. New York: M. H. Newman & Co., 1850.
         (M 1549.4 B798A)

4. Bradbury, W. B.   Bright Jewels for the Sunday School. New York:
         Bigelow & Main, 1869. (M 2193 B798b)

5. Bradbury, W. B.   Daniel, or The Captivity and Restoration. A Sacred
         cantata. New York: Mason Bros., 1854. (M 2062 B724)

6. Bradbury, W. B.   Flora's Festival: A musical recreation for schools,
         etc. New York: M. H. Newman & Co., 1847. (M 1996 B798F)

7. Bradbury, W. B.   The Golden Censer: A musical offering to the Sabbath
         Schools. New York: W. B. Bradbury, 1864. (M 2193 B798gc)

8. Bradbury, W. B.   Golden Chain of Sabbath School Melodies. New York:
         Ivison, Phinney & Co., 1861. (M 2193 B798g)

9. Bradbury, W. B.   Golden Shower of Sunday School Melodies. Rochester,
         N.Y.: E. Darrow & Bro., 1862. (M 2193 B798gs)

10. Bradbury, W. B.   The Jubilee: An extensive collection of church music
         for the choir, the congregation, and the singing-school. Also, the
         sacred cantata, Esther, The Beautiful Queen. New York: Mason Bros.,
         1857. (M 2121 B798j)

11. Bradbury, W. B.   The Key-Note. New York: Mason Bros., 1863.
         (M 2121 B798k)

12. Bradbury, W. B.   The Metropolitan Glee Book. New York: Newman & Ivi-
         son, 1852. (M 1549 B798M)

13. Bradbury, W. B.   The Psalmodist. New York: M. H. Newman, 1844.
        (M 2121 H358Ps)

14. Bradbury, W. B.   The Singing Bird; Progressive music reader. New York:
        Ivison, Phinney & Co., 1852. (M 1994 B798s)

15. Bradbury, W. B.   The Young Melodist; A collection of social, moral and
        patriotic songs. New York: M. H. Newman, 1846. (M 1997 B798y)

16. Hastings, T.   The Manhattan Collection of Psalm and Hymn Tunes and
        Anthems. New York: Ezra Collier & Co., 1838. (M 2121 H358M)

17. Hastings, T.   Musica Sacra: or Springfield and Utica collections
        united. By S. Warriner and T. Hastings. Utica: W. Williams, 1819.
        (M 2116 H358M.2)

18. Hastings, T.   The New York Choralist: Collection of psalm and hymn
        tunes. By T. Hastings and W. B. Bradbury. New York: M. J. Newman &
        Co., 1877. (M 2121 H358N)

19. Hastings, T., ed.   The Presbyterian Psalmodist. Philadelphia: Presby-
        terian Board of Publication, 1852. (M 2130 H358)

20. Hastings, T.   Selah: A collection of Psalm and Hymn Tunes. New
        York: A. S. Barnes & Co., 1856. (M 2121 H358s)

21. Jackson, G. K.   The Choral Companion. Boston: Ezra Lincoln, 1817.
        (M 2116 J122c)

22. Mason, L. and G. J. Webb. Cantica Laudia. New York: Mason and Law, 1850.
        (M 2121 M39ca)

23. Mason, L.   The Choir. Boston: J. H. Wilkins and R. B. Carter,
        1834. (M 2121 M39ch)

24. Mason, L.   The Boston Handel and Haydn Society Collection.
        Boston: Richardson & Lord, 1822. (M 2121 H236) Fourth edition, 1826.
        (M 2121 H236.4)

25. Mason, L. and E. Eves, Jr. The Juvenile Lyre. Boston: J. H. Wilkins and
        R. B. Carter, 1836. (M 1997 M398j)

26. Mason, L.   The Hallelujah. Boston: Mason Bros., 1854.
        (M 2121 M39H)

27. Mason, L.   The Juvenile Singing School. Boston: J. H. Wilkins &
        R. B. Carter, 1843. (MT 935 M399j)

28. Mason, L.   Lyra Sacra. Boston: Richardson, Lord and Holbrook,
        1832. (M 2121 M39L)

29. Mason, L.   Manual of the Boston Academy of Music, 2nd edition.
        Boston: J. H. Wilkins and R. B. Carter, 1836. (MT 10 M299m.2) Many
        editions.

30. Mason, L.   The Modern Psalmist. Boston: J. H. Wilkins & R. B.
        Carter, 1841. (M 2121 M39m)

31. Mason, L.   Musical Exercises for Singing Schools. Boston:
        Kidder and Wright, 1838. (MT 10 M399mu)

32. Mason, L.   New Carmina Sacra. New York: Mason Bro., 1860.
       (M 2121 M39n)

33. Mason, L. and G. J. Webb. The Psaltery. Boston: Wilkins, Carter & Co.,
       1845. (M 2121 M39P)

34. Mason, L.   The Sabbath Hymn Book. New York: Mason Bros.;
       Boston: Mason & Hamlin, 1858. (M 2121 S114M)

35. Mason, L.   The Song-Garden. A series of school music books.
       Boston: Ditson & Co., 1864. (M 1994 M399s.2)

36. Mason, L. and T. Hastings. Spiritual Songs. Boston: Carter, Hendee & Co.,
       1834. (M 2121 H358sp)

37. Merriman, W. T.   The School Song Book, containing a selection of social,
       moral, and patriotic songs. Rochester, N.Y.: Sage & Brother, 1847.
       (MT 935 M571.2)

38. Pratt, G. W. and J. C. Johnson. The Pestalozzian School Song Book. Boston:
       G. P. Reed & Co., 1853. (M 1994 P914)

39. Shaw, O.   For the Gentlemen. (Photostat) Dedham, Mass.: H.
       Mann, 1807. (M 177 S535)

40. Shaw, O.   For the Gentlemen. For woodwind quartet, ed. R.
       Smith. New York: Mercury Music Corp., 1947. (Score and parts)
       (M 457 S535f)

41. Shaw, O.   Melodia Sacra. Providence: Miller and Hutchens, 1819.
       (M 2116 S535M)

42. Shaw, O.   The Providence Selection of Psalm and Hymn Tunes.
       Dedham: Printed by H. Mann and Co. for the author, 1815. (M 2116 S535P)

43. Shaw, O.   The Social Sacred Melodist. Providence: the author,
       1835. (M 1999 S535)

44. Shaw, O.   Thanksgiving Anthem. Dedham: printed and sold by H.
       Mann for the author, 1809. (M 2077 S535)

45. Webb, G. J. and L. Mason. The Boston Chorus Book. Boston: Wilkins, Carter,
       & Co., 1846. (M 2006 M399B)

46. Webb, G. J.   The Common School Songster. Boston: Jenks and Palmer,
       1842. (M 1994 W366)

47. Woodbury, I. B. and B. F. Baker. The Boston Musical Education Society's
       Collection of Church Music. Boston: Saxton, Pierce and Co., 1843.
       (M 2121 B167Bo.6)

48. Woodbury, I. B. and B. F. Baker. The Choral. A collection of church music.
       Boston: Otis, Broaders & Co., 1847. (M 2121 B167c)

49. Woodbury, I. B.   The Dulcimer: or the New York collection of sacred
       music. Boston: W. J. Reynolds and Co., 1850. (M 2121 W884du)

50. Woodbury, I. B.   The Cythara. New York: F. J. Huntington & Mason
       Bros., 1854. (M 2121 W884c)

51. Woodbury, I. B.   The Settlement of Jamestown, selected from the most

celebrated operas. . . by the author, 1856. (M 1548 W884s)

Records

Composer and Title	Recording	ESM No.
1. Jackson, G. K.		
a. Dirge for General Washington	Vic LM-57	LP 712
2. Webb, G. J.		
a. Song over a child	Vic LM-57	LP 712

From The Easy Instructor by Little and Smith, c. 1798
(See Outline VIII)

THE
BOSTON HANDEL AND HAYDN SOCIETY
COLLECTION OF CHURCH MUSIC.

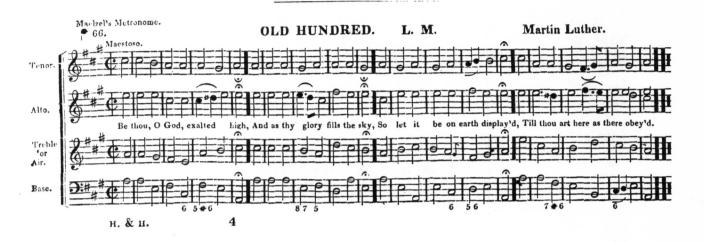

A page from the fourth edition of 1826 by Lowell Mason

From <u>The Choir</u> by Lowell Mason, 1834

Original edition of
"From Greenland's Icy Mountains" by Lowell Mason, 1824

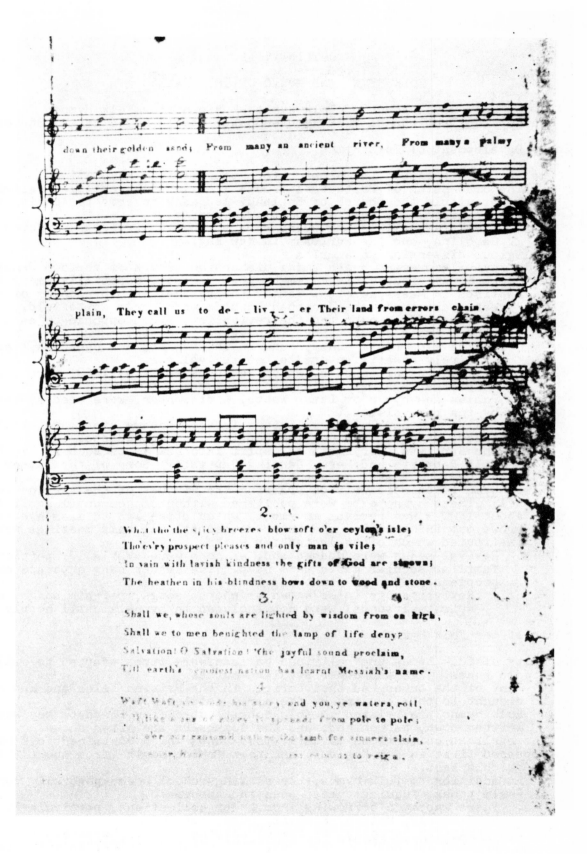

down their golden sands; From many an ancient river, From many a palmy

plain, They call us to de—liv——er Their land from errors chain.

2.

What tho' the spicy breezes blow soft o'er ceylon's isle;
Tho'ev'ry prospect pleases and only man is vile;
In vain with lavish kindness the gifts of God are strewn;
The heathen in his blindness bows down to wood and stone.

3.

Shall we, whose souls are lighted by wisdom from on high,
Shall we to men benighted the lamp of life deny?
Salvation! O Salvation! the joyful sound proclaim,
Till earth's remotest nation has learnt Messiah's name.

4.

Waft Waft, ye winds his story and you, ye waters, roll,
Till like a sea of glory it spreads from pole to pole;
Till o'er our ransom'd nature the lamb for sinners slain,
Redeemer, king, creator, in bliss returns to reign.

OUTLINE VIII

FOLK HYMNS AND MUSIC OF THE SHAKERS

Early Development of Folk Hymns--Music of the Folk Hymns
Southern Collections of Folk Hymns--Gospel Songs--Music of the Shakers

I.   Early Development of Folk Hymns

     A. Religious dissension in Europe before the American Revolution.
         1. The dissension of Protestant groups with institutionalized religion,
             particularly the Church of England, led many to come to America to
             gain religious as well as political freedom.
             a. The Episcopalians, however, were strong in Virginia and North
                 Carolina, and the Puritans in New England.
     B. Religious dissension in America.
         1. A revival movement began among dissension groups of various denomina-
             tions in America. This movement grew rapidly, especially among the
             Baptists in Massachusetts. Among the evangelistic preachers of the
             "Great Awakening" were Jonathan Edwards and George Whitefield.
             a. The orthodox groups and the revivalists stood opposed to each
                 other, among other things, in regard to music.
                 1) The slow Psalm tunes, sung in the New England churches, were en-
                     tirely unsatisfactory to the revivalists.
                 2) The singing schools, which began as early as 1720, were also a
                     protest against New England Psalmody.
             b. Psalms and hymns by Isaac Watts, a dissenter, were used as texts
                 by the revivalists.
         2. Following the Revolution religious freedom became even more widely
             realized, especially among the Baptists and Methodists.
             a. The Baptists, for instance, split into new sects such as the Free
                 Will Baptists and Merry Dancing Baptists. Some of the latter
                 joined the Shaker movement.
             b. Hymn texts were written praising the virtues of the various sects.
                 1) These hymn texts were published without tunes until about 1805.
         3. About 1800 a new revival movement, which often led to mass hysteria,
             broke out in Kentucky, and inter-denominational camp meetings were
             instituted which often lasted for weeks.
             a. Revival songs were needed and, as none were available, portions of
                 familiar secular music were used. The leader sang a phrase and the
                 people repeated the text and tune.
                 1) Revival songs (also known as chorus songs, refrain songs, or
                     spiritual songs) were not included in hymnals until nearly 1840.

II. Music of the Folk Hymns

     A. Texts of folk hymns and religious ballads were first adapted to ballads,
         fiddle tunes, jigs and other secular sources.
         1. Many of the tunes had their origin in the British Isles and had been
             brought to this country by the early settlers.
         2. Folk hymns are related to folk songs, but differ in that they were
             written down, harmonized, and the composers are often known.
     B. The earliest collections of harmonized tunes which contained folk hymns
         appeared first in New England, and then in the South (from about 1810)
         and Middle West.
         1. In addition to folk hymns, the singing-school books generally contained
             Psalm tunes, fuguing tunes, odes and anthems.
             a. There was much borrowing from other collections, particularly those
                 by Billings, Holden, Kimball, Swan, Tans'ur.
         2. The Christian Harmonist by Samuel Holyoke (Salem, Massachusetts, 1804).
             a. Written for Baptist churches. It contained folk-like music set to

folk texts, but was used only in New England.
3. The Christian Harmony or Songster's Companion by Jeremiah Ingalls
   (Exeter, New Hampshire, 1805) (M 7).
   a. This collection contained 80 tunes with texts. It was not much
      used in New England, however, but became popular in the South.
C. Notation (shape-notes, patent-notes, buckwheat notes, character notes).
   1. Most of the early hymnals were printed in the four-shape system (38
      collections were published before 1856).
      a. The four syllables used (faw, sol, law, mi) are given in Morley's A
         Plaine and Easie Introduction to Practicall Musicke, 1597 (p. 6).
   2. Collections using the four-shape system followed the notation de-
      veloped by William Little and William Smith in The Easy Instructor
      (1798) (M 10). Andrew Law's system used the same four syllables, but
      with a square for "faw" and a triangle for "law" and without the use
      of a staff. Little and Smith's notation was as follows:

          C   D   E   F   G   A   B   C

         faw sol law faw sol law mi faw

      a. "Flat" keys were minor and "sharp" keys were major.
      b. The scale began with "faw" in every "sharp" key and with "law" in
         every "flat" key.
      c. The note values were the same as in conventional notation.
      d. The order of voices was treble (top line), counter (using the alto
         "cliff"), tenor (singing the melody), bass.
      e. The parts were all written on separate staffs.
      f. Accidentals were rarely used in shape-note notation.
   3. Seven-shape system
      a. As early as 1832 an effort was made to introduce a seven-shape
         system. In 1846, J. B. Aikin published The Christian Minstrel in
         Philadelphia. He used seven different shapes with the syllables
         do, re, mi, fa, sol, la, si. This system is still used today.
      b. A variety of shape-notes were used in different collections
         (B 12, p. 337).
      c. The seven-shape system at first paralleled, but has now generally
         replaced the four-shape system, except in the Southern Harmony and
         the Original Sacred Harp.
         1) Hymnals of the Southern Baptist Church are now published in both
            the seven-shape and conventional notation.
D. Characteristics of musical style
   1. The music was largely in three parts at first, but alto parts were
      soon added to many of the songs.
      a. All parts except the bass were sung by both men and women, result-
         ing in four real parts with the upper three doubled at the octave.
   2. Melody
      a. The melody was in the tenor, except when the word "Air" was printed
         before the top staff.
      b. Many melodies are pentatonic.
         1) Fourth and seventh degrees omitted in major.
         2) Second and sixth degrees omitted in minor.
      c. Hexatonic melodies omit the fourth or seventh degree in major and
         the sixth in minor.
      d. Ionian, Aeolian, Mixolydian, Dorian modes are found.
      e. Tunes printed in minor are often sung modally, and even in major,
         the singers altering the notes by ear. The use of the Aeolian
         minor is frequent.
      f. Repetition of characteristic melodic figures is common. Melodies
         are often of wide range.
      g. Second and third phrases are sometimes similar (A B B' A;

                    A B B' C)
                    1) Other forms: A B; A A A' B; A A' B C; A B A C; A B C D.
            h. Non-harmonic passing tones used.
            i. Melodic intervals larger than fifth are rarely found, except be-
                tween phrases.
        3. Harmony
            a. The so-called "dispersed harmony" often has parallel fifths and
                octaves, even in the outer parts.
            b. Consonant intervals are fourths, fifths, octaves.
            c. The third is frequently omitted in final cadences.
            d. Half cadences often occur on a chord in second inversion.
            e. Modulation is very rare.
            f. The theoretical principles of William Tans'ur (c. 1706-1783) were
                the basis of many of the "Rudiments of Music" given in the shape-
                note hymnals.
        4. Counterpoint
            a. Primitive form of counterpoint with attempts at canonic imitation.
            b. Dissonance sometimes results from independent lines.
    E. Manner of singing
        1. The leader "pitches out" the song (gives the tonic pitch) and it is
            first sung with the syllables, then with the text. The singers often
            beat time with an up and down motion similar to the "tactus" in Re-
            naissance music. No accompaniment is used.
        2. Singing schools were organized by a travelling "singing master" and
            lasted one or two weeks. The singing master taught the people how to
            read music with the aid of the four syllables and usually used his
            own collection of music.
        3. Numerous singing conventions were organized to provide opportunity
            for massed singing.
            a. Only a few still remain, including those in Benton, Kentucky;
                Birmingham, Alabama; Atlanta, Georgia.
            b. The usual procedure at a convention today is to sing every song in
                the book before any song is repeated; "all day singing with dinner
                on the ground."
        4. Ornamentation
            a. Melodies are freely ornamented.
            b. The singer often adds a high, or a low, grace note before going to
                a lower melody note.
            c. At the end of a phrase a leap of an octave might be taken falsetto.
            d. Frequent use of slides, scoops, anticipations.
            e. Coloring of intervals by the singers sometimes results in "neutral
                thirds."
        5. Meter
            a. The meter is often free in performance. Sometimes to give the
                singer a chance to breathe; or because of the use of ornamentation;
                the greater importance of the words; the adaptation of an old tune
                to new words.
            b. The variations in interpretation of the same tune are often re-
                flected in the printed versions during the period 1810-1840.

III. Southern Collections of Folk Hymns in Four-shape Notation

    A. Repository of Sacred Music, Part Second by John Wyeth (Harrisburg, Penn-
        sylvania, 1813) (P 7)
        1. This collection, although not published in the South, was a source
            for many harmonized tunes used in Southern folk hymnody.
    B. Kentucky Harmony was compiled by Ananias Davisson (1780-1857), a singing
        master, and published in Harrisonburg, Virginia, about 1815. It was the
        first Southern collection to contain harmonized tunes.
        1. It was the source for many folk hymns found in later collections and
            also included anthems and other pieces, suitable for singing schools.

C. The Missouri Harmony (1820) by A. D. Carden. (M 4; M 2; M 23, p. 152)
   1. Settings are mostly in four parts, and sixteen pages are devoted to the "Grounds and Rudiments of Music."
   2. Folk-hymns, Psalm tunes, anthems, and a supplement are included in the edition of 1846.
   3. Folk-hymns include Consolation (p. 25), Rockbridge (p. 22), Ninety-Third (p. 31), Glasgow (p. 47), Morality (p.54).
   4. The compiler "acknowledges himself indebted to Mr.'Wyeth's Repository, part second' for many of the rules and remarks." (M 4, p. 12)

D. The Southern Harmony, and Musical Companion (1835) (M 28; M 2)
   1. William Walker, A. S. H. (Author of Southern Harmony) (1809-1875) was the compiler of this collection and harmonizer of many of the tunes. He was of Welsh descent and lived in Spartanburg, South Carolina, where he became known as "singin' Billy." His Southern Harmony became exceedingly popular in singing schools, especially in the rural sections of the South.
      a. Walker's last edition of Kentucky Harmony, which still used the four-shape system, was in 1854. He published Christian Harmony after the Civil War in the seven shape-note system, but it did not become popular.
   2. The 355 songs (mostly in three parts) in the collection are principally folk hymns with a few "Psalms" and "Odes and Anthems."
      a. Many of the songs were used in the Sacred Harp (1844).
      b. An unusual feature of the notation is the use of ⊃ or ⧿ for 4/4 time, but sung two beats in a bar.
   3. Many songs are taken from The Missouri Harmony and other collections.
      a. "Captain Kidd" (p. 50; Missouri Harmony p. 57) retained the title of the ballad describing the hanging of Captain Kidd in 1701.
      b. "Evening Shade" (p. 46; Missouri Harmony p. 56) was a popular "fuguing tune."
      c. "Happy Land"(p. 89) is a hexatonic melody with the fourth omitted.
   4. "The Good Old Way" (p. 156) by William Walker is an example of a revival song with a chorus refrain.
   5. Ornamentation of melodies may be seen in "Kedron" (p. 3) and the "Ninety-Third Psalm" (p. 7).

E. Original Sacred Harp (Denson Revision) (M 20; M 2)
   1. The Sacred Harp by B. F. White and E. J. King was published in Philadelphia in 1844. This collection contained much material from earlier shape-note collections, particularly Walker's Southern Harmony, and was widely used. The fifth edition of the Sacred Harp (1911) was revised and enlarged by Joe S. James.
   2. The "Denson Revision" was based on the fifth edition by James.
      a. Many of the early Sacred Harp songs, however, were restored and a number of newly composed fuguing tunes were added. Many of the less popular songs were omitted.
   3. The music, written in four-shape notation, is mostly in four parts.
      a. Some of the borrowed music which was originally in three parts has had the fourth part (alto) added.
      b. The tunes are given to the tenor voice as in other collections.
      c. Dyadic harmony used in pentatonic folk hymns (P 4)
   4. Melodies borrowed from secular sources.
      a. "Sweet Affliction" (p. 145) uses the well-known song "Go tell Aunt Tabby" for the first half of the melody.
      b. "Soft Music" (p.323) is based on "Du, du liegst mir im Herzen."
      c. "Plenary" (p. 162) is "Auld Lang Syne."
   5. Modal melodies
      a. "Shepherds Rejoice" (p. 152), Ionian.
      b. "Golden Harp" (p. 274), Aeolian.
      c. "The Converted Thief" (p. 44), Mixolydian.
      d. "Wondrous Love" (p. 159), Dorian (the D-flat is sung as D-natural).
      e. "The Hebrew Children" (p. 133), Phrygian (rare).

      6. Pentatonic melodies
        a. "New Britain" (p. 45), fourth and seventh omitted.
        b. "Restoration" (p. 312), second and sixth omitted.
      7. Hexatonic melodies
        a. "Tribulation" (p. 29), sixth omitted.
        b. "Primrose" (p. 47), seventh omitted.
  F. Other collections of four-shape hymn books (list in <u>White Spirituals</u> by George Pullen Jackson, <u>B</u> 12: p. 25).
    1. <u>Choral-Music</u> by Joseph Funk (Harrisonburg, Virginia, 1816).
    2. <u>The Methodist Harmonist</u> by B. Waugh and T. Mason (New York, <u>c</u>. 1821) (<u>M</u> 14).
    3. <u>The Ohio Sacred Harp</u> by Lowell Mason and Timothy Mason (Cincinnati, Ohio, 1834).
    4. <u>The Harmonist</u> by T. Mason and G. Lane (New York, 1837) (<u>M</u> 6).
    5. <u>Union Harmony</u> by William Caldwell (Maryville, Tennessee, 1837).
    6. <u>Hesperian Harp</u> by William Hauser (Philadelphia, 1848).
    7. <u>Social Harp</u> by J. G. McCurry (Philadelphia, 1855).
  G. Collections of seven-shape nymn books (list in <u>White Spirituals</u> by George Pullen Jackson, <u>B</u> 12: p. 323).
    1. <u>Norristown New and Improved Music Teacher</u> by D. Somer (Norristown, Pennsylvania, 1832).
    2. <u>Christian Minstrel</u> by Jesse B. Aikin (Philadelphia, 1846).
    3. <u>Harp of Columbia</u> by W. H. and M. L. Swan (Knoxville, Tennesse, 1848).
    4. <u>Christian Harmony</u> by William Walker (Philadelphia, 1866).
    5. <u>The New Harp of Columbia</u> by M. L. Swan (Nashville, Tennessee, 1867).
      a. Modern edition published by M. E. Church, South, Nashville, Tennesse, 1936.
    6. <u>Olive Leaf</u> by William B. Houser (Philadelphia, 1878).
  H. Contemporary composers have made use of folk hymns, fuguing tunes and folk tunes.
    1. Randall Thompson (<u>The Peaceable Kingdom</u>); Van Denman Thompson (<u>The Evangel of the New World</u>); John Powell (<u>Natchez on the Hill</u>; <u>A Set of Three</u>); Roy Harris (<u>Folk Song Symphony</u>); Virgil Thomson (<u>The River</u>); Henry Cowell, Thomas Canning and many others.

II. Gospel Songs

  A. Although at first only different in notation, the music in the seven shapes gradually changed in character as well.
    1. Music now printed in the seven shapes is largely of the worst sort, combining a "gospel" text with stereotyped music having a catchy rhythmic movement.
    2. Thousands of copies of collections of gospel songs are published annually in the South. Singing schools, taught by the compilers of the collections, are being held today in rural sections of the South and West.
      a. The "Blessed Hope" collection (<u>M</u> 1) uses the following shape-notes. These are the same as in Aikin's collection of 1846.

      △   ▽   ◇   ◁   ◯   ▢   ◊
      do re mi fa sol la ti

  B. Composers and song leaders
    1. Charles C. Converse (1832-1918), "What a Friend We Have in Jesus"; William H. Doane (1832-1915), "Saved by the Blood of the Lamb"; William G. Fischer (1835-1912), "I Love to Tell the Story"; Hart P. Danks (1834-1903), "Silver Threads among the Gold," "Not Ashamed of Christ"; Philip P. Bliss (1838-1876), "Rescue the Perishing"; Ira D. Sankey (1840-1908), "The Ninety and Nine"; Homer Rodeheaver (1880-   ), "Brighten the Corner Where You Are."

III. Music of the Shakers (1776-1876)

    A. History of Shakerism
        1. Originated in English Quaker Church and the earlier "French Prophets"
            or Camisards. The religious beliefs of these revivalists included
            violent bodily motions.
            a. They were known as the "United Society of Believers in Christ's
                Second Appearing," "Shaking Quakers," and as "Shakers."
        2. The Society of Shakers was founded in 1772 by Ann Lee, called "Mother
            Ann."
        3. Ann and eight followers came to America in 1774 and in 1776 finally
            settled in Watervliet (Niskeyuna), New York.
            a. Religious revivalism was prevalent at that time, and Shakerism
                spread to New England and Eastern New York (the central church was
                at New Lebanon, N. Y.). After 1800, communities were established
                in Kentucky and Ohio (one near Cleveland on Shaker Heights).
                1) Attempts were made to establish communities at Mount Morris
                    (later Son Yea), N. Y., and Sodus, N. Y. (1826).
            b. Of the seventeen Societies established, only three remain today
                (1955). These are at Sabbathday Lake (New Gloucester), Maine;
                Canterbury, N. H.; and Hancock, Massachusetts.
            c. The Shaker brothers and sisters lived separately on communal farms.
                They made furniture and other household articles and developed many
                labor-saving devices. Even a simple task was a consecrated act.
    B. Religious beliefs
        1. The Shakers believed in Divine revelation, the millenium, celibacy,
            formal confession, separation and equality of the sexes, and in the
            second coming of Christ (in the person of Ann Lee, a masculine-
            feminine Deity).
        2. Dancing and bodily movement were considered to be an act of praise and
            a part of Divine worship.
            a. Marches and dance songs were sung to express the "inner spirit."
                The "Holy Squares," filled with symbolism, were their highest
                dance ritual.
        3. Between 1830-1860 the ritual was most colorful and the public was in-
            vited to the services. Persecution and ridicule, however, eventually
            led to the closing of the services to all except Believers.
    C. Shaker music (B 1; P 1)
        1. Early tunes were sometimes derived from New England Psalmody and many
            religious and secular tunes were adapted or rewritten by the few who
            knew music.
            a. The earliest hymnal known was written in 1807, but the songs and
                dances go back to 1781.
            b. Gradually the songs became more lively and folk-like and some Eng-
                lish folk-tunes appeared.
        2. During the Great Revival (1837-1847) "gifts" began to be "received"
            by the laity, both young and old, through "visions."
            a. The "gifts" included songs, messages, and presents from the spirit
                world.
            b. The "visions" were accompanied by shaking, whirling, and dancing
                and came from Mother Lee, the Saviour, Saints and Angels.
            c. The songs "received" were notated in manuscript books and learned
                by the congregations by rote.
                1) Some tunes had metrical form, but many were meaningless repeti-
                    tions of short phrases or syllables. Tunes were frequently the
                    basis for improvisation.
                2) Some songs were "received" from Indian, Negro and Chinese
                    spirits as well as in unknown tongues.
        3. Instrumental music was not allowed; the Shaker voice was "God-given
            and God-tuned."
    D. Notation
        1. The first known tune-books were written in the usual round-note

notation.

2. An attempt at a new musical notation was made about 1820, when singing classes were organized.
   a. Various types of letter notation were experimented with, including
      shape-notes, and a method was finally standardized at New Lebanon.
3. The first seven letters of the alphabet were used.
   a. Whole note - A
   b. Half note - a'
   c. Quarter note - _a
   d. Eighth note - ă
   e. Sixteenth note - ẵ
4. Meter (mode) was indicated by special signs at the beginning of the
piece: ‖ = 4/4; ╫ = 2/4; ╫ = 3/4; ‖ = 6/8; ₵ = 3/8
   a. Some tunes changed meter frequently. ₵
5. Tempo was indicated by the numbers 1 to 4.
   a. 1 - Adagio; 2 - Largo; 3 - Allegro; 4 - Presto.
   b. The tempo was determined by a "speediometer." "A bullet attached
      to a string 39 1/2 inches long will very nearly vibrate seconds."
   c. Various lengths were given for various tempos.
6. All major scales had c for a basic note; all minor scales had d for a
basic note (Dorian).
7. Harmonized tunes were rare until after 1860.

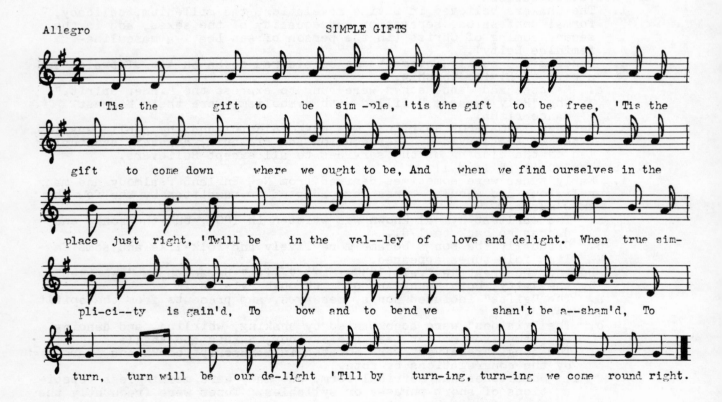

Allegro   SIMPLE GIFTS

Allegro   COME LIFE, SHAKER LIFE

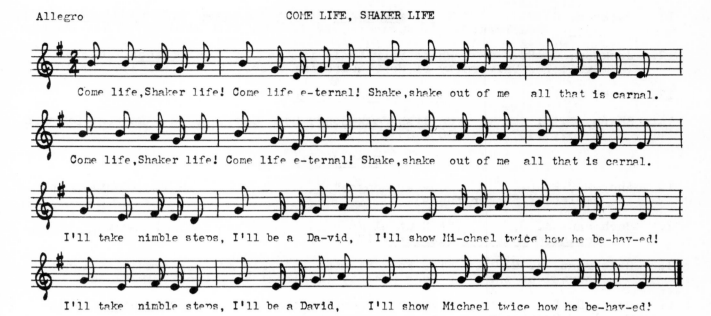

Come life, Shaker life! Come life e-ternal! Shake, shake out of me   all that is carnal.

Come life, Shaker life! Come life e-ternal! Shake, shake   out of me   all that is carnal.

I'll take   nimble steps, I'll be a Da-vid,   I'll show Mi-chael twice how he be-hav-ed!

I'll take   nimble steps, I'll be a David,   I'll show Michael twice how he be-hav-ed!

BIBLIOGRAPHY

Books

The publications of George Pullen Jackson should be consulted in connection with the folk hymn.

1. Andrews, E. D.   The Gift to be Simple. Songs, Dances and Rituals of the American Shakers. New York: J. J. Augustin, 1940. Contains many examples of Shaker tunes. (M 2131.S4 A566)

2. Brown, T.   An Account of the People Called Shakers. Troy, N.Y.: Parker and Bliss, 1812. (M 2131.S4 B881)

3. Ellinwood, L.   The History of American Church Music. New York: More-house-Gorham Co., 1953. (ML 200 E46)

4. Gilfillan, A.   Singing Schools in America. ESM Thesis, 1939.

5. Herzog, G.   Research in Primitive and Folk Music in the United States. Washington, D. C.: American Council of Learned Societies, Bulletin No. 24 (April, 1936). (ML 3551 H582)

6. Horn, D. D.   Shape-Note Hymnals and the Art Music of Early America. ESM Thesis, 1942.

7. Horn, D. D.   A Study of the Folk-Hymns of Southeastern America. ESM Dissertation. 1953.

8. Jackson, G. P.   Another Sheaf of White Spirituals. Gainesville: University of Florida Press, 1952. (ML 3551 J122)

9. Jackson, G. P.   Early Songs of Uncle Sam.   Boston: Bruce Humphries, 1933. (ML 3551 J121)

10. Jackson, G. P.   The Story of the Sacred Harp, 1844-1944. Nashville:
     Vanderbilt University Press, 1944. (ML 3111 J13)

11. Jackson, G. P.   White and Negro Spirituals, Their Life Span and Kin-
     ship. New York: J. J. Augustin, 1943. (ML 3551 J12w)

12. Jackson, G. P.   White Spirituals in the Southern Uplands. Chapel
     Hill: The University of North Carolina Press, 1933. (ML 3551 J12)

13. Mack, J. P.   Music of the Shakers. ESM Essay, 1952.

14. Sharp, C. J.   English Folk-Song, Some Conclusions. London: Simpkin
     & Co., 1907. (ML 3652 S53)

Periodicals

1.   Andrews, E. D.   "Shaker Songs," MQ XXIII (1937), 491. (Contains ex-
     amples of Shaker tunes)

2.   Buchanan, A. M.   "A Neutral Mode in Anglo-American Folk Music,"
     Southern Folklore Quarterly IV, p. 77.

3.   Gilchrist, A. G.   "The Folk Element in Early Revival Hymns and Tunes,"
     Journal of the Folk Song Society (England) VIII (Dec., 1928), 61.

4.   Horn, D. D.   "Dyadic Harmony in the Sacred Harp," Southern Folk-
     lore Quarterly IX, No. 4 (Dec., 1945).

5.   Horn, D. D.   "Shape-Note Hymnals and the Art Music of Early
     America," Southern Folklore Quarterly V, No. 4 (Dec., 1941).

6.   Jackson, G. P.   "Buckwheat Notes," MQ XIX (1933), 393.

7.   Lowens, I.   "John Wyeth's Repository of Sacred Music, Part
     Second: A Northern Precursor of Southern Folk Hymnody," JAMS V (1952),
     114.

8.   Metcalf, J.   "The Easy Instructor," MQ XXIII (1937).

9.   Reichenbach, H.   "The Tonality of English and Gaelic Folksong," ML
     XIX (1938), 269.

10. Seeger, C.   "Contrapuntal Style in the Three-Voice Shape-Note
     Hymns," MQ XXVI (1940), 482.

Music

1.   Blessed Hope. Dallas, Texas: Stamps-Baxter Music and Printing Co., 1942.

2.   Buchanan, A. M.   Folk Hymns of America. New York: J. Fischer, 1938.

3.   Buchanan, C.   Early American Hymn Tunes (1800-1860). Music by L.P.
     Breedlove, S. Jenks, J.P. and S.R. Penick, J.P. Reese, W. Walker and
     anonymous composers. New York: Music Press, 1942. (M 2079.E43 B919)

4.   Carden, A. D.   The Missouri Harmony. Cincinnati: Phillips and Rey-
     nolds, 1846. (M 2121 M678)

5.   Copland, A.   Old American Songs. New York: Boosey and Hawkes.

6.   The Harmonist. New York: T. Mason and G. Lane, 1837. (M 2127 M288.2)

7. Ingalls, J.   Northfield, ed. Lowens. New York: E. B. Marks, 1954.

8. Jackson, G. P.   Down-East Spirituals and Others. Three hundred songs
        supplementary to Spiritual Folk-Songs of Early America. New York: J. J.
        Augustin, 1937. (M 1629 J122d)

9. Jackson, G. P.   Spiritual Folk-Songs of Early America. New York: J.
        J. Augustin, 1937. Contains 250 tunes and texts. (M 1629 J122s)

10. Little, W., and W. Smith. The Easy Instructor. Albany: Websters and Skin-
        ner and Daniel Steele, 1798? (M 2116 L728.2). Selection from The
        Easy Instructor: Exhortation by E. Doolittle. Philadelphia: Elkan-
        Vogel Co., 1954.

11. Lomax, A., and J. A. Lomax. American Ballads and Folk Songs. New York: The
        Macmillan Co., 1934. (M 1629 L839A)

12. Lomax, A., and J. A. Lomax. Folk Song in U. S. A. New York: Duell, Sloan &
        Pearce, 1947. (M 1629 L839f)

13. McDowell, L. L.   Songs of the Old Camp Ground. Ann Arbor, Mich.:
        Edwards Bros., 1937. (M 1658 T29M13)

14. The Methodist Harmonist. New York: B. Waugh and T. Mason, for The Method-
        ist Episcopal Church, 1833. (M 2127 M592.2)

15. Niles, J. J.   Ten Christmas Carols from the Southern Appalachian
        Mountains. New York: G. Schirmer, 1935. (M 2065 N698t)

16. Niles, J. J.   Seven Kentucky Mountain Tunes. New York: G. Schirmer,
        1929. (M 1658 K37N69)

17. Niles, J. J.   More Songs of the Hill-Folk. New York: G. Schirmer,
        1936.

18. Niles, J. J.   Songs of the Hill-Folk. New York: G. Schirmer, 1934.
        (M 1629 N698Soh)

19. Old American Folk Songs. The Old Harp Singers of Nashville, Tennessee.
        New York: J. Fischer and Bro., 1934.

20. Original Sacred Harp. (Denson Revision). Haleyville, Alabama: Sacred Harp
        Publishing Co., 1936. (M 2121 S1233)

21. Powell, J.   Five Virginian Folk Songs. New York: J. Fischer and
        Bro., 1934. (M 1668.1 V81P88)

22. Powell, J.   Twelve Folk Hymns. New York: J. Fischer and Bro.,
        1934. (M 1668.1 P884)

23. Sandburg, C.   The American Songbag. New York: Harcourt, Brace &
        Co., 1927. (M 1629 S213A.2)

24. Sharp, C. J.   English Folk Songs from the Southern Appalachians. 2
        vols. London: Oxford University Press, 1932. (M 1668.1 S53E)

25. Sharp, C. J.   Folk-Songs of English Origin. Collected in the
        Appalachian Mountains. London: Novello & Co., 1918. (M 1668.1 S53f)

26. Smith, H.   The Church Harmony. Chambersburg, Pa.(Henry Ruby,
        1831. Contains Psalm and Hymn tunes in four shape-note notation.

        (M 2121 S649)

27. Smith, R., and H. Rufty. <u>American Anthology of Old World Ballads</u>. New
        York: J. Fischer, 1937.

28. Walker, W.   <u>The Southern Harmony</u>. New Haven, Conn.: 1835. Re-
        production of 1854 edition was made in 1939 by Federal Writers Pro-
        ject. (M 2117 W186s)

29. Weber, T. R.   <u>Die Pennsylvanische Choral Harmonie</u>. Allentown, Pa.:
        Blumer & Bush, 1844. Text in German and English. Four shape-note
        notation. (M 2121 W376)

Records

<u>Title</u>	<u>Recording</u>	<u>ESM No.</u>
1. <u>Bayou Ballads of the Louisiana Plantations</u>	Vic M-728	A 622
a. Marianne's Loves		
b. When Your Potato's Done		
c. Suzanne, Suzanne, Pretty Girl		
d. Forward March, Grenadiers		
e. Poor Little Mamzelle Zizi		
f. Come Dance Codaine		
g. Clementine		
h. You Are a Blacamoor		
i. Lullaby		
j. Ah! Suzette Dear		
k. Zelim Thou Hast Left the Cane Field		
l. Sing, Sweet Bird		
2. <u>Catholic Mission Music in California</u>	New Rec 2001	LP 497
a. Missa de Los Angeles a 4 (1796)		
b. Si Quaeris miracula		
c. Cántico Espiritual		
d. Alabado (Tenor and chorus)		
e. Alabado (Women's voices)		
f. Santa Dios (Traditional)		
3. Copland, A.		
a. <u>Appalachian Spring</u>. Shaker tune "The Gift	Van VRS-439	LP 1145
to Be Simple" used at No. 55 in the orchestral		
score (M 1003 C784Am)		
4. <u>Early American Carols</u> (Arr. by J. J. Niles)	Disc 732	A 810
a. The Seven Joys of Mary		
b. The Little Liking		
c. Natthew, Mark, Luke and John		
d. I Wonder as I Wander		
e. The Carol of the Birds		
f. The Carol of the Angels		
5. <u>Early American Carols and Folk Songs</u> (Arr. by	Vic M-718	A 22
J. J. Niles)		
a. Jesus, Jesus, Rest Your Head		
b. When Jesus Lived in Galilee		
c. Down in the Forest		
d. Jesus, the Christ is Born		
e. See Jesus the Saviour		
f. The Cherry Tree		
g. Who Killed Cock Robin		

          h.   The Old Woman and the Pig
          i.   The Frog Went Courting
          j.   The Carrion Crow

6.   Five Sea Chanties (Arr. by C. Dougherty)   Col ML-2206   LP 713
          a.   Rio Grande
          b.   Blow Ye Winds
          c.   Across the Western Ocean
          d.   Mobile Bay
          e.   Shenandoah

7.   Folk Music of the U. S. (11 vols.)   Library of   A 715-725
                                                   Congress

8.   Folk Songs and Ballads (Susan Reed)   Vic M-1107   A 842

9.   Old American Songs (William Warfield)   Col ML-2206   LP 713
          (Arr. by Aaron Copland)
          a.   The Boatman's Dance (Minstrel Song, 1843)
          b.   The Dodger (Campaign Song)
          c.   Long Time Ago (Ballad)
          d.   Simple Gifts (Shaker Song)
          e.   I Bought Me a Cat (Children's Song)

10.   Old Colony Times (c. 1800)   Col M-329   A 599

11.   Old World Ballad in America   Col M-408   A 621
          (Ed. by A. R. Summers)
          a.   The Cherry Tree Carol
          b.   Old Bangum
          c.   The Ballad of Mary Hamilton
          d.   The Hangman's Tree
          e.   The Two Sisters
          f.   Barbara Allen
          g.   The Lady Gay

12.   Old Harp Singing   Folkways FP-56

13.   Pound, E. T.
          a.   The Loved Ones (from the "Sacred Harp")   Col M-329   A 599

14.   Sacred Harp Singing (Folk Music in the United   Library of   A 725
          States, vol. XI). Music in The Original   Congress, XI
          Sacred Harp (M 22).

15.   The Songs of Early America   Bost ES-1   A 533
          a.   The Saint's Delight (Early White Spiritual)
          b.   Bird's Courting Song (Children's Ballad)
          c.   Dewy Dens of Yarrow (Early Ballad)
          d.   The Devil and the Farmer's Wife (Early Ballad)
          e.   Fare You Well My Own True Love (Early Ballad)
          f.   Soldier Won't You Marry Me? (Answer-Back Song)
          g.   Five Dollars a Day (Sea Chantey)
          h.   The Unconstant Lover (Pioneer Song)
          i.   Lubly Fan (Early Minstrel Song, 1844)

16.   Susan Reed in Folk Songs   Col ML-54368   LP 351
          a.   Sweet Betsy from Pike (Westward Movement)
          b.   Turtle Dove (Southern Mountain)
          c.   Next Market Day (Irish)
          d.   The Riddle Song (American)

    e.   The Zebra Dun (Cowboy Song)
    f.   Gentle Johny, My Jingalo (Old English)
    g.   My Lagan Love (Irish)
    h.   Molly Malone (Irish)
    i.   Fare Thee Well (Southern Mountain)

AN OFFERING OF PRAISE.

To the altar of truth holy offerings I'll bring, And a
song of sweet praise I will loudly sing: For my spirit is fill-
ed with heavenly joy, And the praises of God shall my
tongue employ.

2 Through the loud sounding trump I'll proclaim the glad word,
  Heaven's arches resound while I praise the Lord;
  For the gates of salvation are open to me,—
  I will shout and I'll sing, praise the Lord! I am free.

3 In the regions of bliss I have found an abode,
  I am owned of my Savior, O praise the Lord!
  I am free to acknowledge my good Mother Ann,
  For I'm saved by her word,—praise the Lord! Amen.

                              Canterbury, N. H

A Shaker hymn from
A Sacred Repository of Anthems and Hymns, 1852

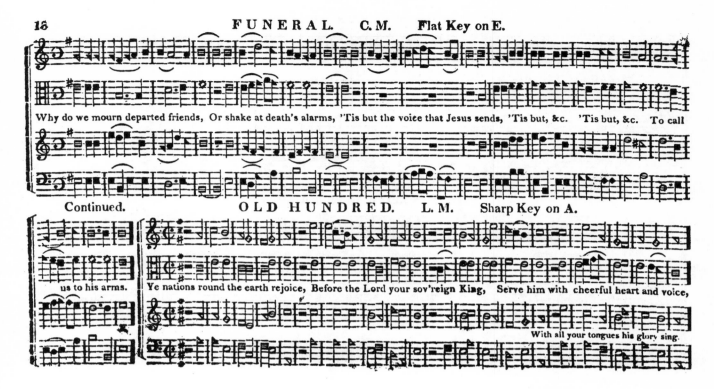

From <u>The Easy Instructor</u> by Little and Smith, <u>c</u>. 1798

From <u>The Missouri Harmony</u> by Allen D. Carden, 1846

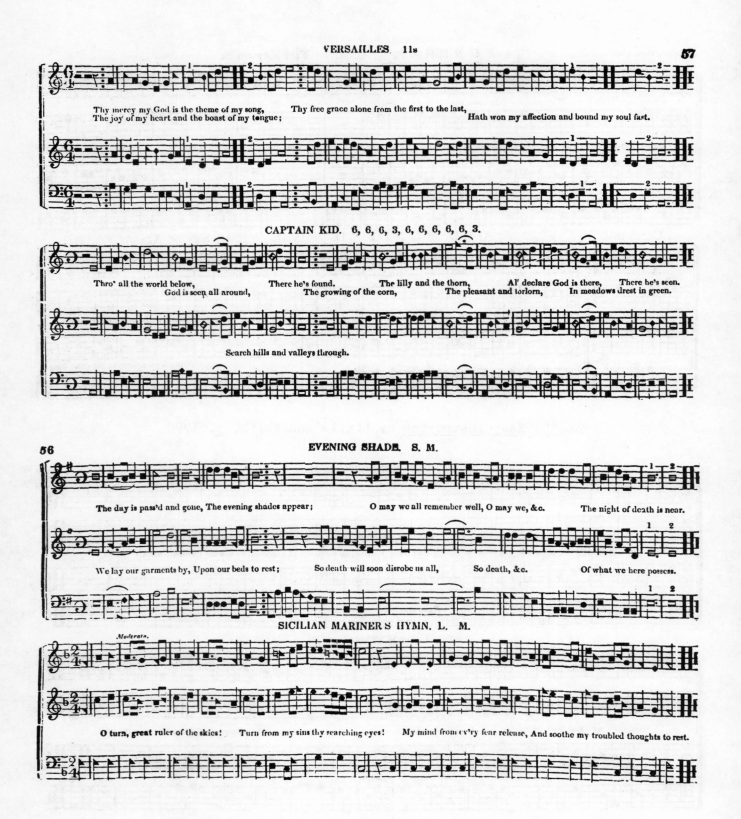

From The Missouri Harmony by Allen D. Carden, 1846

Obs. 1. Care should be taken that all the parts (when singing together) begin upon their proper pitch. If they are too high, difficulty in the performance, and perhaps discords will be the consequence; if too low, dullness and langour. If the parts are not united by their corresponding degrees, the whole piece may be run into confusion and jargon before it ends, and perhaps the whole occasioned by an error in the pitch of one or more parts, of only one semitone.

2. Each one should sing so soft, as not to drown the teacher's voice; and each part so soft, as will permit the other parts to be distinctly heard. If the teacher's voice cannot be heard, it cannot be imitated; and if the singers of any one part are so loud that they cannot hear the other parts because of their own noise, the parts are surely not rightly proportioned, and ought to be altered.

3. The bass should be sounded full and bold; the tenor regular and distinct; the counter clear and plain, and the treble soft and mild, but not faint. The tenor and treble may consider the German flute, the sound of which they may endeavor to imitate if they wish to improve the voice.

4. The high notes, quick notes, and slurred notes, of each part, should be performed than the low notes, long notes, and single notes of the same parts.

5. Learners should sing all parts somewhat softer than their leaders do, as it tends to cultivate the voice, and give an opportunity of following in a piece with which they are not well acquainted: but a good voice may be soon much injured by singing too loud.

6. All the notes included by one slur, should be sung at one breath if possible.

7. All notes (except some in syncopation) should be fairly articulated; and in applying the words, great care should be taken that they be properly pronounced, and not torn in pieces between the teeth. Let the mouth be freely opened, the sound come from the lungs,* and not be entirely formed where they should be only distinguished, viz: on the end of the tongue. The superiority of vocal to instrumental music is, that while one only pleases the ear, the other informs the understanding.

8. When notes of the tenor fall below those of the bass in sound, the tenor should be sounded full and strong and the bass soft.

9. There are but few long notes in any tune, but what might be swelled with propriety. The swell is one of the greatest ornaments to vocal music, if rightly performed. All long notes of the bass should be swelled, if the other parts are singing short or quick notes at the same time. The swell should be struck plain upon the first part of the note, increase to the middle and then decrease or die away like the sound of a bell.

*The organs of a man's voice (or the lungs) is in form somewhat like a tube, about one fourth of an inch in diameter, and possesses power sufficient to divide a note or tone of music into one hundred equal parts.

10. The common method of beating the two first modes of common time is as follows: for the first beat, bring down the end of the fingers to whatever is used for beating upon; for the second bring down the heal of the hand; for the third, raise the hand a few inches; and for the fourth, raise the hand up nearly as high as the shoulder in readiness for the next measure.

For the triple time mood, let the two first be the same as the two first of common time; and for the third, raise the hand a little higher than for the third beat of common time, when it will be in readiness for the next measure.

For the third and fourth moods of common time, and the two moods of compound time, there is just one motion down and one up for each measure; with this difference, for the common time moods there is no resting for the hand; but in compound time, the resting is double the length of the motion.

11. Learners should beat by a pendulum, or by counting seconds, until they can beat regular time, before they attempt to beat and sing both at once; because it perplexes them to beat, name and time the notes all at once, until they have acquired a knowledge of each by itself.

12. While first learning a tune, it may be sung somewhat slower than the mood of time requires, until the notes can be named, and truly sounded without looking on the book.

13. Some teachers are in the habit of singing too long with their pupils. It is better to sing but six or eight tunes at one time, and inform the learners concerning the nature and disposition of the pieces, and the manner in which they should be performed, and continue at them until they are understood, than to skim over 40 or 50 in one evening, and at the end of a quarter of schooling, perhaps few, besides the teacher, know a flat keyed piece from a sharp keyed one; what part of the anthems, &c. require an emphasis; or how to give the pitch of any tune which they have been learning, unless some person informs them. It is easy to name the notes of the piece, but it requires attention and practice to sing one.

14. Too long singing at one time, injures the lungs.†

15. I have found by experience, that learners will soon know when to sing soft and when strong, if they are led, by the teacher making a larger motion in beating where emphatical words or notes occur, than where others do.

†A cold or cough, all kinds of spirituous liquors, violent exercise, bile upon the stomach, long fasting, the veins overcharged with impure blood, &c. &c. are destructive to the voice of one who is much in the habit of singing. A frequent use of spirituous liquors will speedily ruin the best voice.

A frequent use of some acid drink, such as purified cider, elixir of vitriol with water vinegar, &c. if used sparingly are strengthening to the lungs.

From <u>The Missouri Harmony</u> by Allen D. Carden, 1846

56   EVENING SHADE. S. M.

The day is pass'd and gone, The evening shades appear;   O may we all remember well, O may we, &c.   The night of death is near.

We lay our garments by, Upon our beds to rest;   So death will soon disrobe us all,   So death, &c.   Of what we here possess.

SICILIAN MARINER'S HYMN. L. M.

Moderato.

O turn, great ruler of the skies!   Turn from my sins thy searching eyes!   My mind from ev'ry fear release, And soothe my troubled thoughts to rest.

From <u>The Missouri Harmony</u> by Allen D. Carden, 1846

The selfdenying Way.

3 Lord, may I with submission bow, And bend unto thy holy will. May I be humble, meek and low, And my internal foes repel.

Lord, may I watch my steps with care, Nor from the path of virtue stray. May I the seamless robe prepare. This is a self denying way.

2 Love and union is the object All believers should pursue: Give up ev'ry other project; Keep the heav'nly prize in view.

From the holy church of Zion Lo the voice of wisdom cries, Love and union, love and union, Love and union is the prize.

A fervent Petition.

O Lord, in thy heavenly kingdom of glory I long to appear both spotless and holy. I want to join those in their blessed devotion,

Who by the true power of God are in motion. Fill me with thy power, fill me with thy love. O feed me with manna from

heaven above; And let thy rich blessings eternally flow; That in me the fruits of the Gospel may grow.

Brought from Harvard in the year 1827.

2. Fill me with that fire which burns up old nature; That I may adore my God & Creator. Let this blessed fire enliven my spirit; That I may the Gospel's pure treasure inherit. Let me stand unshaken, when trials I feel. Lord, give me a lively and heavenly zeal, To press for the mark, for that beautiful prize, that unspotted crown that's laid up for the wise.

Dedication. Sung at the dedication of the Meeting house, in July, 1828.

3. Now we with joyful consolation Have appear'd before the Lord. Let us in songs of adoration, Sound the praises of our God.

And while the just do here assemble, Worship God with honest hearts, Let ev'ry sinner fear & tremble, Nor assume the scoffer's part.

The faithful Shepherd.

I am your faithful Shepherd; I've watch'd for your increase. And in the hour of danger I watch you round with peace.

I have prepar'd a mansion For you my little flock, And plac'd you all in order Upon the solid rock.

Three Shaker Hymns in manuscript

OUTLINE IX

SECULAR MUSIC (1800-1860)

Concert Life--Song Composers--Stephen Foster
Louis Gottschalk--John S. Dwight

I. Concert Life

   A. Philadelphia, Boston and New York were centers of musical entertainment
      in early 19th century.
      1. Concerts included songs and ballads, operatic selections, orchestral
         pieces and instrumental solos.
   B. Musical Societies, formed by the leading musicians, helped to raise the
      musical standards.
      1. The Philharmonic Society was organized largely as the result of the
         efforts of U. C. Hill (1802-1875), a Connecticut violinist. He
         played in the orchestra until 1875 and conducted a few of the concerts.
         a. The first program, given in Apollo Rooms on Dec. 7, 1842, included
            Beethoven's Fifth Symphony, Weber's Overture to Oberon, Kalliwoda's
            Overture, Hummel's Quintette, vocal excerpts from Oberon, Beetho-
            ven's Fidelio, Mozart's Belmont and Constantia, and a duet from
            Rossini's Armida. Madame Otto and C. E. Horn were the vocalists.
   C. The outstanding foreign concert pianists, Henry Christian Timm (1811-
      1892), Daniel Schlesinger (1799-1839), William Scharfenberg (1819-1895),
      were active in the musical life of New York from the 1830's.
   D. Operas by Rossini, Weber, Paisiello, Bellini, Donizetti, excerpts from
      Tannhäuser, Handel's Messiah (1831), and Mendelssohn's St. Paul (1838),
      were heard in New York in the first half of the 19th century.
      1. Lorenzo da Ponte (1749-1838), Mozart's librettist (Le nozze di Figaro,
         Cosi fan tutte, Don Giovanni) was active in New York from 1805. In
         1833 an opera house was built as the result of his efforts.

II. Song Composers

   A. Concerts of ballads and popular songs were a favorite type of musical
      entertainment, and foreign and American composers wrote a large number
      of these songs.
      1. C. E. Horn (1786-1849)
         a. Came from London in 1833 and was active in Boston and New York as
            a singer, pianist and composer of opera, oratorio and songs.
         b. He and his wife were prominent in ballad concerts and often ap-
            peared on concert programs given by others.
         c. Music: EMCS pp. 3, 6
      2. Joseph P. Knight (1812-1887)
         a. English organist and song composer. Although only in the United
            States from 1839-41, he met with great popular success.
         b. His best known song, written in the United States, is "Rocked in
            the Cradle of the Deep." (EMCS pp. 8, 11)
      3. Henry Russell (1812-1900)
         a. Came to America in 1833 and became organist of the First Presby-
            terian Church in Rochester, N.Y. He then settled in New York, re-
            turning to England in 1841.
         b. His best known songs are "Woodman, Spare that Tree," and "The Old
            Arm Chair."
         c. Music: EMCS pp. 13, 17
      4. John H. Hewitt (1801-1890)
         a. American-born son of James Hewitt, he played an important part in
            the musical life of his time. He is known today for his ballad
            "All Quiet along the Potomac."
         b. Music: EMCS pp. 28, 31, 34

    5. Septimus Winner (Alice Hawthorne) (1827-1902)
       a. Known for his songs "Listen to the Mocking Bird" (EMCS p. 42) and "Whispering Hope."
       b. He wrote "methods" for many instruments, including the accordion, concertina, reed organ, clarionet, fife flute, piccolo, piano-forte, and guitar.
    6. Minstrel shows were becoming increasingly popular and Negro minstrel songs, mostly in imitation of the Negro's style of singing, appeared in large numbers. Dan Emmett (1815-1904), the composer of "Dixie," and E. P. Christy were prominent in the field. Christy introduced, sometimes under his own name, many of the songs of Stephen Foster.
       a. Music: M 1; M 2

III. Stephen Collins Foster (1825-1864)

  A. Life
    1. Foster was born near Pittsburgh of well-to-do parents. His only interest was in writing songs, and he failed as a student and was unsuccessful in business. Even after his songs achieved great popularity, he was unable or unwilling to protect his rights. He led a troubled existence and died in poverty at the age of 38. His purse contained just thirty-eight cents and a piece of paper with the pencilled words "Dear friends and gentle hearts."
  B. Music
    1. He wrote 201 songs and instrumental pieces, all in the major mode. Most of these were featured in minstrel shows, particularly Christy's. They reveal his great gift for melody and are sometimes gay, sometimes sentimental, and always simply harmonized. The songs achieved great popularity and some of the more familiar ones, such as "Old Folks at Home" (1851), "Oh! Susanna" (1848), "My Old Kentucky Home" (1853), have become true folksongs. One of his last songs was "Beautiful Dreamer."
       a. His basic harmonic background is often I-IV-V-I, or merely the alteration of I-V with secondary chords occasionally appearing.
       b. Other patterns are I-IV-I-V (half cadence) I-IV-I-V-I.
    2. Music: M 3-10

IV. Louis Moreau Gottschalk (1829-1869)
  A. One of the first American virtuosi. He was born in New Orleans; died in Rio de Janeiro and is buried in Brooklyn. He studied piano and composition in Paris from 1841 to 1846; toured France, Switzerland and Spain and spent six years in the West Indies. He returned to America in 1853 and made many tours throughout the United States, playing and conducting his own works. He appeared in Rochester in 1864 and 1865. His eccentric manner, showy technique, and sentimental compositions made him extraordinarily popular, especially with the ladies.
  B. Music: "The Last Hope," "The Dying Poet," "The Banjo" (M 11)

V. John S. Dwight (1813-1893)
  A. Dwight was an American musician and critic of high standards. He graduated from Harvard in 1832 and later became a Unitarian minister. He was one of the founders of the Harvard Musical Association (1837) (not connected with Harvard University), which is still active.
  B. In 1852 he established his Journal of Music, which was published until 1881. It is a most important source for music and musical events during that period.
    1. A number of attempts had been made in New England to found periodicals devoted to music, but none survived more than a few years (P 4).
       a. Euterpeiad. Boston, 1820-1823
       b. Lyre. New York, 1824-1825
       c. Euterpeiad. New York, 1830-1831

   d. The Musical Review. New York, 1838
   e. Boston Musical Gazette. Boston, 1838-1846
   f. Musical World. New York, 1849-1860

BIBLIOGRAPHY

Books

1. Claghorne, C. E.   The Mocking Bird; the Life and Diary of It's Author,
      Septimus Winner. Philadelphia: The Magee Press, 1937.

2. Cooke, G. W.   John Sullivan Dwight. Boston: Small, Maynard and
      Co., 1898. (ML 423 D99C77)

3. Dwight, J. S.   Dwight's Journal of Music. John S. Dwight, editor.
      1852-1881. (ML 1 D992)

4. Erskine, J.   The Philharmonic Symphony Society of New York. Its
      First Hundred Years. New York: The Macmillan Co., 1943.
      (ML 200.8 N5E73)

5. Ewen, D.   Music Comes to America. New York: Thomas Y Crowell
      Co., 1942. (ML 200 E94)   (EwenMCA)

6. Fors, L. R.   Louis Moreau Gottschalk. Havana: La Propaganda Lit-
      eraria, ;880. (ML 410 G68F)

7. Foster, M.   My Brother Stephen. Indianapolis, Ind.: Privately
      printed for the Foster Hall Collection, 1932. (ML 410 F757F75)

8. Gottschalk, M.   Notes of a Pianist (trans. by Robert Peterson).
      Philadelphia: Presser, 1891. (ML 410 G68G6)

9. Hoffman, R.   Some Musical Recollections of Fifty Years. New York:
      Charlee Scribner's Sons, 1910. (ML 417 H711)

10. Howard, J. T.   Stephen Foster, America's Troubadour. New York:
      Thomas Y. Crowell Co., 1934. (ML 410 F757H84)

11. Huneker, C.   The Philharmonic Society of New York. A Retrospect.
      Privately printed. (ML 200.8 N5H93P)

12. Johnson, D. L.   The Use of Instruments in the Worship Service in New
      England Churches from Colonial Days to about 1850. ESM Thesis, 1953.

13. Milligan, H. V.   Stephen Collins Foster, A Biography. New York: G.
      Schirmer, 1920. (ML 410 F757M65)

14. Morneweck, E. F.   Chronicles of Stephen Foster's Family. Pittsburgh,
      Pa.: Pittsburgh University Press, 1944. (ML 410 F757M6c)

15. Ponte, L. da   Memoirs. New York: Houghton Mifflin, 1929.
      (ML 423 P813s)

16. Russell, H.   Cheer! Boys, Cheer! Memories of Men and Music.
      London: J. Macqueen, 1895. (ML 420 R96)

17. Seymour, M. A. I.   Life and Letters of Louis Moreau Gottschalk. By
      Octavia Hensel pseud. Boston: O. Ditson & Co., 1870. (ML 410 G68S52)

18. Sonneck, O. G.   Catalogue of the First Editions of Stephen C. Foster.

Washington: Library of Congress, Government Printing Office, 1915.
(ML 134 F75W6)

19. Walters, R.   Stephen Foster: Youth's Golden Gleam; A sketch of his
     life and background in Cincinnati. Princeton, N.J.: Princeton Univer-
     sity Press, 1936. (ML 410 F757W23)

Periodicals

1. Howard, J. T.   "Louis Moreau Gottschalk, as Portrayed by Himself,"
     MQ XVIII (1932), 120.

2. Howard, J. T.   "Newly Discovered Fosteriana," MQ XXI (1935), 17.

3. Jackson, G. P.   "Stephen Foster's Debt to American Folksong," MQ
     XXII (1936), 154.

4. Johnson, H. F.   "Early New England Periodicals Devoted to Music,"
     MQ XXVI (1940), 153.

5. Waters, E. N.   "John Sullivan Dwight, First American Critic of Music,"
     MQ XXI (1935), 69.

Music

1. Christy, E. P.   The Christy's Minstrels Song Book. Three vols. in
     one. London: Boosey & Co., 187-? (M 1497 C55)

2. Christy, E. P.   Christy's Panorama Songster. New York: W. H. Murphy,
     185-? (M 1365 C556)

3. Foster, S. C.   The Foster Choral Book, ed. by W. A. Fisher. Boston:
     Ditson Co., Inc., 1936. (M 1548 F757)

4. Foster, S. C.   Foster Hall Reproductions, Songs, compositions and ar-
     rangements by Stephen Foster, 1826-1864. Indianapolis, Ind.: Kirby
     Lilly, 1933. (M 3 F757)

5. Foster, S. C.   Minstrel Songs, Old and New. Boston: Ditson Co.,
     1882. (M 1670 M66)

6. Foster, S. C.   Negro Minstrel Melodies, ed. by H. T. Burleigh.
     New York: Schirmer, 1909. (M 1670 D96n)

7. Foster, S. C.   A Program of Stephen Foster Songs, ed. and arr. by
     J. T. Howard. New York: J. Fischer & Bro., 1934. (M 1629 F757)

8. Foster, S. C.   Songs and Musical Compositions of Stephen C. Foster.
     In biography of Morrison Foster. Pittsburgh: Percy F. Smith, 1896.
     (M 1629 F756)

9. Foster, S. C.   The Songs of Stephen Foster, ed. by A. E. Wier. New
     York: Harcourt, Brace and Co., 1935. (M 1620 F757W64)

10. Foster, S. C.   A Village Festival. New York: Edition Musicus, 1946.
     (M 462 F757v)

11. Gottschalk, L. M.   Piano Works, Vols. 1-13. Mayence: Schott & Son,
     187-. Boston: Oliver Ditson, 1886. (M 22 G78G)

12. Howard, J. T.   A Program of Early and Mid-Nineteenth Century Songs.

(Music by Horn, Knight, Russell, Baker, Clifton, Hewitt). New York: J.
Fischer and Bro., 1931. (M 1629 H849) (EMCS)

13. Winner, S.   Accordeon Method, Winner's improved; containing the
rudiments of music.... Philadelphia: C. H. Davis, Winner and Schuster,
1854. (MT 680 W776a)

14. Winner, S.   New Method for Reed Organ or Melodeon.... Cleveland:
S. Brainard's Sons, 1877. (MT 202 W776)

15. Winner, S.   Winner's New Method for the Pianoforte. Cleveland:
S. Brainard's Sons, 1872. (MT 746 W776)

Records

Composer and Title	Recording	ESM No.
1. Baker, J. C.		
a. The Burman Lover (1847)	Col M-329	A 599
2. Foster, S. C,		
a. Ah, May the Red Rose Live Alway	Col ML-2108	LP 256
b. Album of Songs (Crooks)	Vic M-554	A 748
1) Old Folks at Home		
2) Beautiful Dreamer		
3) My Old Kentucky Home		
4) Come Where My Love Lies Dreaming		
5) Oh! Susanna		
6) Old Black Joe		
7) I Dream of Jeanie with the Light Brown Hair		
8) Massa's in de Cold Ground		
9) Ah! May the Red Rose Live Alway		
10) De Camptown Races		
c. Carry me Back to Old Virginny (Anderson)	Vic LM-1703	LP 1348
d. Foster Gallery (arr. Gould)	Vic M-727	A 314
e. I Dream of Jeanie (Murphy)	Vic 4010	R 245
f. I Dream of Jeanie (Warfield)	Col AAL-32	LP 29
g. My Old Kentucky Home (Anderson & Piatigorsky)	Vic LM-1703	LP 1348
h. Oh! Boys, Carry Me 'Long (Homer)	Vic 87309	R 321
i. Oh! Susanna (arr. Clokey)	Col M-329	A 599
j. Oh! Susanna (Crane)	Vic 22616	R 1416
k. Old Black Joe (Neilsen)	Col 37184	R 840
l. Old Folks at Home (Traubel)	Col M-639	A 1436
m. Village Festival and Old Folks Quadrilles	ARS 15	LP 1170
(Arr. from Foster's The Social Orchestra by		
Lowell and Kay)		
1) Stop that Knocking at the Door		
2) Way Down in My Heart I've Got a Feeling		
for You		
3) Somebody's Grandpa		
4) History ob de World		
5) Nelly Bly		
6) Angel Gabriel		
3. Gottschalk, L. M.		
a. Cakewalk (arr. Kay)	Col ML-4616	LP 815
4. Pound, E. T.		
a. The Loved Ones (1859)	Col M-329	A 599

5. Winner, S.
   a. Listen to the Mocking Bird (1865)   Col M-329   A 599
       (arr. Clokey)

6. Gottschalk, L. M.
   a. March of the Gibares   All 3024   ELP 69

The Germania Musical Society in 1853

From the original edition of
"My Old Kentucky Home, Good-Night!" by Stephen Foster, 1852

OUTLINE X

FOREIGN MUSICIANS ABOUT 1850

Musical Life--Foreign Virtuosi--The German Influence--Louis A. Jullien

I. Musical Life

    A. There was a real musical life in most of the larger cities by the middle
        of the 19th century. The sensational foreign virtuosi who came over
        about that time achieved great success, especially in the western cities
        where not much music had been heard.
        1. Concerts, except in the larger centers, were generally regarded as a
            popular entertainment, sometimes on the level of a minstrel show or
            circus, and eccentric personalities were exploited.

II. Foreign Virtuosi

    A. Violinists
        1. Ole Bull (1810-1880)
            a. Born in Bergen, Norway; studied violin with Spohr and was strongly
                influenced by Paganini.
            b. He made five very successful tours of the United States between
                1843-1879. In 1852 he attempted to establish a Norwegian colony
                in Potter County, Pennsylvania, called "Oleana."
            c. He developed an unusual style of playing with an almost level
                bridge and flat fingerboard, which enabled him to play all four
                strings at once. At a concert in Rochester, N.Y. in 1844 one
                number was a "Quartette, composed for four instruments, and per-
                formed on one, by Ole Bull."
            d. His concerts consisted mostly of his own compositions and arrange-
                ments, and his spectacular and bizarre style attracted an enthu-
                siastic public.
            e. Music: M 2-4
        2. Edward Remenyi (1830-1898)
            a. Born in Hungary; studied violin with Böhm at the Vienna Conserva-
                tory; banished from Austria for participation in the Hungarian
                Revolution of 1848; became solo violinist to Queen Victoria (1854);
                appointed solo violinist to the Emperor of Austria (1860).
            b. In 1865 he began a series of long tours which took him to France,
                Germany, Belgium, Holland, England, United States, Canada, Mexico,
                Japan, China and the Cape of Good Hope. He died during his last
                American tour.
            c. Rémenyi had a brilliant technique and is said to have played with
                vigor and passion. He made skillful transcriptions of compositions
                by Bach, Schubert, Chopin and others, and composed a violin con-
                certo and solo violin pieces.
    B. Pianists
        1. Henri Herz (1806-1888)
            a. Born in Vienna; studied there and in Germany and Paris; later be-
                came a professor at the Paris Conservatory (1842-1874); began his
                tours in 1831; toured the United States, Mexico and West Indies
                (1845-51).
            b. He was known as a brilliant performer and was a fashionable teacher
                and composer. His florid piano compositions (over 200) catered
                entirely to popular taste.
            c. Music: M 5-8
        2. Sigismund Thalberg (1812-1871)
            a. Born in Geneva; studied in Vienna with Hummel and others; began
                concert tours in 1830; appointed court pianist at Vienna (1834);
                toured the United States in 1856.
            b. He was a brilliant, but superficial pianist and was at his best as

an interpreter of salon-music.
  1) A feature of his pianistic style, widely imitated, was to play
     a central melody with the thumb of either hand, surrounding it
     with brilliant figurations.
  c. Music: M 9, 10
C. Singers
  1. Maria Malibran (1808-1836)
     a. Born in Manchester, England; daughter of the Spaniard, Manuel
        García, with whom she studied; became a famous dramatic contralto;
        made her operatic debut in London (1825).
     b. She came to New York with her father and became a popular favorite,
        singing in Italian operas (1825-1827).
  2. Henriette Sontag (1806-1854)
     a. Born in Koblenz; became a famous dramatic soprano and coloratura
        singer; sang in opera in Vienna and the soprano solos in the
        first performance of Beethoven's Missa Solemnis and Ninth Sym-
        phony (Vienna, 1824).
     b. She sang in New York (1852-1853) in opera and concerts with sensa-
        tional success.
  3. Jenny Lind (1820-1887)
     a. Born in Stockholm; became a world-famous soprano; known as the
        "Swedish Nightingale." She made her debut in opera in 1838;
        studied with Manuel García in Paris (1841) and with her London
        debut (1847) she reached the pinnacle of her fame.
     b. She toured the United States in 1850-1852 from East to West with
        P. T. Barnum, the showman, as her manager. He exploited her as he
        did his circus attractions, and she soon became a sensation. She
        is said to have received a guarantee of $150,000 for 150 concerts.
     c. Jenny Lind's first concert in America was given September 11, 1850.
        A prize of $200 had been offered by Mr. Barnum for a song to be
        called "Greeting to America." Tickets for the concert were sold at
        auction. The first ticket was bought by a hatmaker for $225. The
        total sale was over $25,000, and Jenny Lind contributed $10,000 of
        this amount to charity.
        1) In spite of some nervousness at the beginning of the concert,
           Jenny had a tremendous success and was ranked by the New York
           press as the foremost artist who had yet visited America.
        2) The program of her first concert was as follows:

CASTLE GARDEN.
First Appearance of Mademoiselle Jenny Lind,
on
WEDNESDAY EVENING, 11th SEPTEMBER, 1850....
Programme.

Part I.

Overture (Oberon,) - - - - - - - - - - - - - - - - - Weber.
Aria "Sorgete," (Maometto Secondo,) - - - - - - - - - Rossini
Signor Belletti.
Scena and Cavatina, "Casta Diva" (Norma)- - - - - - - Bellini.
Mademoiselle Jenny Lind.
Duet on two Piano Fortes,- - - - - - - - - - - - - - -Benedict.
Messieurs Benedict and Hoffman.
Duetto, "Per piacer alla Signora," (Il Turco in Italia,) - - Rossini.
Mademoiselle Jenny Lind and Signor Belleti.

Part II.

Overture, (The Crusaders,) - - - - - - - - - - - - - -Benedict.
Trio for the Voice and two Flutes, composed expressly for

      Mademoiselle Jenny Lind, (Camp of Silesia,) - - Meyerbeer.
              Mademoiselle Jenny Lind.
            Flutes, Messrs. Kyle and Siede.
Cavatina "Largo ad Factotum," Il Barbiere, - - - - - Rossini.
               Signor Belletti.
The Herdsman's Song, more generally known as The Echo Song,
                     Mademoiselle Jenny Lind.
The Welcome to America, written expressly for this occa-
        sion, by Bayard Taylor, Esq. - - - - - - - - Benedict.
             Mademoiselle Jenny Lind.

Conductor, - - - - - - - - - - - - - - - - - - M. Benedict.
The Orchestra will consist of Sixty Performers, including the first
Instrumental talent in the country.
     Price of Tickets Three Dollars. Choice of places will be sold by Auction,
at Castle Garden.
     Doors open at six o'clock. Concert to commence at eight o'clock.
     No checks will be issued.
     Mdlle. Jenny Lind's Second Grand Concert, will be given at Castle Garden,
on Friday evening, 13th instant.
     Chickering's Grand Pianos will be used at the first Concert.

> 3) In Rochester, N. Y., on July 22, 1851, she sang the following
> songs on a mixed program: "Come unto Him" (Messiah), Handel;
> two arias from La Sonnambula, Bellini; "The Bird's Song," Tau-
> bert; "Comin' through the Rye."

II. The German Influence

A. The Revolution in Central Europe in 1848 sent many fine German musicians
    to America. These, in contrast to the virtuosi, came to America to live,
    settling not only in Boston, New York and Philadelphia, but in Cincinnati,
    St. Louis, Milwaukee and other inland cities.
  1. These well-trained musicians dominated American musical life until
      1900 as composers, teachers, solo performers, and in orchestral,
      chamber music and choral groups.
    a. Some of these men were Alfred Jaell, a pupil of Moscheles; Otto
        Dresel, a friend of Schumann; and William Scharfenberg. These
        three played the Concerto for three claviers by Bach in Boston in
        1853 (Dwight's Journal II, 1853, p. 175).
    b. Piano concertos by Mendelssohn (1844) and Chopin (1846) and Mendels-
        sohn's violin concerto (1849) were heard.
  2. The complete dominance of German music affected the native composers,
      who studied with German teachers in this country and often went to
      Germany to complete their education.
    a. A few Americans, however, began to feel that American music was
        being neglected, and some protested against the German dominance
        and the neglect of (and discrimination against) American music.
B. The Germania Musical Society
  1. Twenty-five members came from Berlin to New York in 1848. They de-
      voted themselves to orchestral playing and gave performances of music
      by Wagner, Beethoven, Weber, Spohr, Mozart, Haydn, and Mendelssohn,
      as well as the usual descriptive fantasias for popular appeal.
    a. In 1853 the Society performed the first complete symphony --
        Beethoven's Second -- to be heard in Chicago.
  2. After 6 years (1848-1854) the Society disbanded, and many of the
      musicians became prominent as conductors, teachers, and performers in
      Baltimore, Boston, New York, Philadelphia, Syracuse and Chicago.

III. Louis A. Jullien (1812-1860)

    A. Student at Paris Conservatoire, appeared in London and Paris as conductor, and came to the United States in 1853.

    B. He was a sensational conductor and his programs included music from the classics as well as popular airs.

        1. He conducted Beethoven in white kid gloves and for other important works he used a jewelled baton. Sometimes at a climactic moment he would seize the concertmaster's violin and bow or take a piccolo from his velvet coat and play with the orchestra.

        2. One of his biggest successes was The Fireman's Quadrille during which, as flames burst from the stage, he brought the firemen through the hall with water pouring from the nozzles of their hoses.

    C. Jullien, in spite of his extravagant showmanship, helped in the development of national consciousness through his playing of music by native American composers.

BIBLIOGRAPHY

Books

1. Bull, S. C.   Ole Bull, A Memoir. Boston: Houghton, Mifflin and Co., 1883. (ML 418 B935B93)

2. Carse, A.   The Life of Jullien. Cambridge, England: Heffer, 1951. (ML 422 J94C32)

3. Chaffers, M. R.   Survey of Musical Life in Rochester from 1817 up to the Civil War (1860). ESM Essay, 1947.

4. Chorley, H. F.   Thirty Years' Musical Recollections. London: Hurst and Blackett, 1862. (ML 423 C55t)

5. Chorley, H. F.   Thirty Years' Musical Recollections. New York: Alfred A. Knopf, 1926. (ML 423 C55tn)

6. Dwight, J. S.   Dwight's Journal of Music. John S. Dwight, editor. 1852-1881. (ML 1 D992)

7. Ewen, D.   Music Comes to America. New York: Thomas Y. Crowell Co., 1942. (ML 200 E94)

8. Rosenberg, C. A.   Jenny Lind in America. New York: Stringer and Townsend, 1851. (ML 420 L74R81)

9. Ryan, T.   Recollections of an Old Musician. New York: E. P. Dutton & Co., 1899. (ML 419 R98)

10. Smith, M. B.   The Life of Ole Bull. Princeton: Princeton University Press, 1943. (ML 418 B935S65)

11. Werner, M. R.   P. T. Barnum. New York: Harcourt, Brace & Co., 1923. (ML 429 B263W49)

Periodicals

1. Engel, L.   "Songs of the American Wars," MM XIX (1942), 147.

2. Johnson, H. E.   "The Germania Musical Society," MQ XXXIX (1953), 75.

3. Rogers, F.   "Henriette Sontag in New York," MQ XXVIII (1942), 100.

4. Sabin, R.   "Early American Composers and Critics," <u>MQ</u> XXIV (1938),
        210.

Music

1. Bishop, Sir H. R.   <u>Clari, or the Maid of Milan</u>, an opera in 3 acts.
        (Contains the original "Home Sweet Home"). London: Goulding, D'Almaine
        Potter & Co., 1823. (M 1503 B622C). Also original holograph score of
        the full score.

2. Bull, O.   <u>La Melancolie</u>, for violin and piano. Kjobenhavn: Han-
        sen, 1913. (M 223 B93H)

3. Bull, O.   <u>Saeterjentens söntag</u>. Arr. for string quintet by
        Svendsen. New York: C. Fischer, 1901. (M 552 B93S)

4. Bull, O.   <u>Solitude on the Mountain</u>. Arr. for organ by Saunier.
        Boston: Boston Music Co., 1919. (M 13 B935s)

5. Herz, H.   <u>Collection d'exercices de gammes et de passages pour
        Piano.</u> Leipzig: Peters, 188-? (MT 225 H58)

6. Herz, H.   <u>Collections of Scales and Exercises for the Piano-
        forte.</u> New York: Schirmer, 1894. (MT 231 H582)

7. Herz, H.   <u>Variations et rondeau brillant</u>, 2 pianoforte. Op. 16.
        Leipzig: Hofmeister, 18--. (M 214 H58)

8. Herz, H.   <u>Duo et variations concertans pour piano et violon sur
        la romance, C'est une larme</u>. Paris: I. Pleyel, 182-? (M211 L166d)

9. Thalberg, S.   <u>Home, Sweet Home! Air anglais varie pour le piano</u>,
        Op. 72. New York: G. Schirmer, 1857. (M 39 T365h)

10. Thalberg, S.   <u>Les Capricienses, valses pour le piano</u>, Op. 64.
        Leipzig: Breitkopf & Härtel, 184-. (M 3.3 T365)

Records

Title	Recording	ESM No.
1. Bishop, Sir Henry		
a. Echo Song (Galli-Curci)	Vic 74743	R 2136
b. Home, Sweet Home (Traubel)	Col M-639	A 1436
c. Lo, Here the Gentle Lark (Gluck)	Vic 64267	R 853
(Macbeth)	Col A-5867	R 1896

MUSIC FROM 1850 TO 1900

American Nationalism--Civil War Songs--Music in the West
William Mason--Theodore Thomas--Patrick S. Gilmore
John Philip Sousa--Dudley Buck

I. American Nationalism

    A. Anthony Philip Heinrich (1781-1861)
        1. Although born in Bohemia, this eccentric musician was the first to
            champion the American composer. He came to Lexington, Kentucky, in
            1817 and gave the first performance of a Beethoven symphony -- the
            First -- in America. He returned to Europe at various times before
            settling in New York about 1836.
        2. He considered himself an American and composed songs, piano pieces,
            oratorios and a large number of showy, programmatic orchestral works
            based on American subjects, particularly the Indians and scenic won-
            ders. He was known by his admirers as the "Beethoven of America" and,
            in 1846, conquered New York and Boston with concerts of his own
            compositions.
        3. His program in Boston included the following work:
            TECUMSEH, or The Battle of the Thames -- A martial Ouverture -- for
               full Orchestra.
               Introduction -- the Indian War Council,
               Allegro Eroico -- the Indian War Dance -- Advance of the Americans --
                 Skirmishing -- Battle, and Fall of Tecumseh.
            OUVERTURE -- "To the Pilgrims," -- Full orchestra, with Trumpet Obli-
               gato by Mr. Bartlett, -- comprising the following Tableaux:
            1st -- Adagio Primo, -- The Genius of Freedom slumbering in the
               forest shades of America.
            2nd -- Adagio Secondo, -- She is awakened into life by those moving
               melodies, with which nature regales her votaries in her primeval
               solitude.
            3rd -- Marcia, -- The efforts of power to clip the young eagle of
               liberty.
            4th -- Allegretto Pollaca, -- The joyous reign of universal freedom
               and universal intelligence.
          a. Music: M 6, 7; EMCS p. 1

    B. William Henry Fry (1813-1864)
        1. Grand Opera by foreign composers had been heard in America in the
            early 19th century. Mozart's librettist, da Ponte, was living in
            New York in 1832, and many famous opera singers came from Europe.
        2. Fry, a music critic and composer, wrote the first publicly performed
            grand opera by a native American, Leonora (1845). The libretto is in
            English, but the music, modelled on Meyerbeer and Donizetti, lacks
            distinction and individuality.
        3. He also wrote symphonies (Santa Claus, The Breaking Heart) which were
            played by Jullien, and pled for the recognition of American composers
            by the public.
        4. He claimed that the Philharmonic Society of New York had not played
            a single American work during its first eleven years, a remark which
            began a long controversy.
        5. Music: EMCS p. 45; M 5

    C. George Frederick Bristow (1825-1898)
        1. Born in Brooklyn; violinist in New York Philharmonic Society; composer,
            conductor and organist. He was also a champion of the American
            composer and pointed out that the Philharmonic Society had played only
            one American piece, his own.
          a. The Society made an official statement regarding its policy, which

was that one American work might be performed a season if sub-
mitted to, and approved by, its committee.
2. Bristow was the composer of the second American grand opera, Rip Van
Winkle (1855). Written in light opera style, it is completely undis-
tinguished. Other works include oratorios, symphonies, string quartets, songs, organ, piano and violin pieces.
3. Music: EMCS p. 47; M 1, 2

II. Civil War Songs

A. During the War Between the States (1861-1865) songs were sung every-
where: at home, at camp, and on the battlefield.
B. Dixie was written in 1859 by the minstrel performer, Daniel Emmett
(1815-1904), who was born in Mt. Vernon, Ohio. The song, a "walk-
around" for Dan Bryant's minstrels, became a sensation and was soon
taken over by the Southerners.
C. The Battle Hymn of the Republic, adopted by the Northerners, was written
by Julia Ward Howe in 1861 and set to a tune by the Southerner, William
Steffe. This tune appeared in 1856 and had many different texts, among
them "John Brown's Body."
D. Other well-known Civil War songs
1. Tenting on the Old Camp Ground, by Walter Kittridge, was sung by both
sides.
2. The Battle Cry of Freedom; Just Before the Battle, Mother; and
Tramp, Tramp, Tramp, written by George F. Root (1820-1895) and
Marching Through Georgia by Henry Work (1832-1884).
3. All Quiet Along the Potomac Tonight was written by John H. Hewitt
(1801-1890) who was active in the Confederate cause (EMCS, 34).
Henry Tucker's Weeping, Sad and Lonely, was sung by both the North
and the South.
4. The Bonnie Blue Flag, a marching song by Henry McCarthy, was the
national anthem of the Confederacy (EMCS, 37).
E. Music: M 11, 12, 18, 19

III. Music in the West

A. There was very little music in the West before 1850 except in Chicago,
New Orleans, Cincinnati, St. Louis, and Milwaukee, where Music Societies
had been founded in the earlier part of the century.
B. Concerts, a music school, Music Societies and theatres began to appear
in Chicago after 1833.
1. In 1847 music was in the Chicago public schools, only ten years after
Lowell Mason's system was introduced in Boston.
2. In 1850 grand opera was performed and orchestral music was initiated.
3. Theodore Thomas made his first Chicago appearance in 1869 with his
Central Park Garden Orchestra. San Francisco had opera in 1853.
4. Brahms' Second Symphony, composed in the summer of 1877, was played by
the Musical Society of Milwaukee on December 10, 1878.
C. European virtuosi travelled from east to west in the late 19th century,
but had little influence on the development of native music.
1. In spite of their efforts to play good music, their programs usually
had to include variations on "Yankee Doodle" and other popular airs
("The Arkansas Traveler," "Money Musk"), operatic potpourries, and
sentimental pieces.
    a. Anton Rubinstein (1820-1894) played 215 concerts in the United
    States in 1872-73, but refused to return, even at $2,500 a con-
    cert.
    b. Henri Vieuxtemps (1820-1881) toured the United States in 1872 with
    Rubinstein.
    c. Hans von Bülow (1830-1894) gave 193 concerts in the United States
    in 1875-76.

   d. Henri Wieniawski (1835-1880) toured the United States in 1872
       with Rubinstein.
   e. Teresa Carreño (1853-1917), Venezuelan pianist, made her debut in
       New York in 1862 as a child prodigy. She later studied with
       Gottschalk, Mathias and Rubinstein and also had success as an
       opera singer, composer and conductor. She contributed a great
       deal in securing early appreciation of the music of her pupil,
       Edward MacDowell.

IV. William Mason (1829-1908)

   A. Son of Lowell Mason, William was a leader in the development of American
       music. He was a well-trained musician of high standards and wide ex-
       perience and was a pupil of Liszt at Weimar in 1853. While in Europe he
       met the leading musicians of the day, among them Berlioz, Rubinstein,
       Wieniawski, Joachim, the young Brahms, Rémenyi, Schumann and Wagner.
       1. Mason returned to America in 1854 and began his career as a piano
           virtuoso, giving some of the first serious piano recitals in this
           country. However, he began to devote himself more and more to
           teaching and became the foremost piano teacher of his time.
           a. His piano methods, Touch and Technic (M 10), is still used.

V.   Theodore Thomas (1835-1905)

   A. Thomas came from Germany to New York at the age of nine and helped sup-
       port his family by playing the violin. He played in Jullien's orchestra
       in 1853, and appeared as a concert violinist with Thalberg and others.
       He also played in the Philharmonic in 1854.
   B. In 1862 he organized an orchestra, and through his high standards and
       planned education of the public in good orchestral music, laid the
       foundation for the great orchestras of today.
       1. The first American performance of Wagner's Overture to the Flying
           Dutchman was given.
       2. From 1868 to 1875 he gave his famous series of concerts in Central
           Park Garden.
   C. Beginning in 1869 Thomas travelled from one end of the country to the
       other with his orchestra, and his influence for good music was felt
       everywhere. He met with considerable criticism, however, from those who
       thought he played too much "classical" music.
       1. In Keokuk, Iowa, he conducted a program which included Wagner's Over-
           to Tannhäuser, the second movement of Beethoven's Fifth Symphony and
           Weber's Invitation to the Dance. The latter was arranged for or-
           chestra by Berlioz and a note to this effect was placed under the
           title of the work. The critic of Keokuk, however, interpreted this
           as applying to all three pieces. His review in the local paper the
           next morning was as follows: "The first piece was that fine tri-
           logy which Hector Berlioz with exquisite art made from Wagner,
           Beethoven, and Weber. The thought of Hector Berlioz, evidently, in
           arranging the trilogy was to put after the passionate action of the
           one, the ocean-like, star-like, measureless calm of the symphony.
           After you have bathed in that luxury and languor long enough, there
           comes von Weber's Invitation to the Dance. Oh, there has been no-
           thing heard in Keokuk like this trilogy."
   D. From 1866 he conducted the Brooklyn Philharmonic. In 1872 he helped to
       organize the Cincinnati Festival and became its conductor. In 1877 he
       became conductor of the New York Philharmonic. An effort to establish an
       American Opera Company in New York in 1885 was a financial failure. He
       organized and conducted the Chicago Symphony in 1891.
   E. His programs usually included selections from the classics, works of con-
       temporary American composers and a few pieces of the lighter type. The
       following typical program was given in 1873:

PROGRAMME

PART FIRST

```
OVERTURE        )
SCHERZO         )
INTERMEZZO      ) - Midsummer Night's Dream .............. Mendelssohn
NOCTURNE        )
WEDDING MARCH   )
```

ARIA, "In diesen heil'gen Hallen," Magic Flute .... Mozart
                Mr. Myron W. Whitney

SELECTIONS, 1st Act Lohengrin .... Wagner

OVERTURE, Leonore No. 3 .... Beethoven

SOLO for Harp, Grand Studio, ad imitazione del
    Mandolina .... Parish Alvars
                Mr. A. Lockwood

SONG, A Mariner's Home's the Sea........................ Randegger
                Mr. Myron W. Whitney

WALTZ, Publicisten .... Strauss

OVERTURE, Hunyadi Laszlo .... Erkel

    F. In the last quarter of the 19th century a number of major symphony or-
        chestras were organized.
        1. These included the Boston Symphony (1881), Chicago Symphony (1891), a
            second New York orchestra, the Symphony Society, founded by Leopold
            Damrosch in 1878.
            a. The Symphony Society merged with the New York Philharmonic in 1928.
    G. The Metropolitan Opera was established in 1883.

VI. Patrick Sarsfield Gilmore (1829-1892)

    A. Born in Dublin, Ireland, he went to Canada with a regimental band. He
        later found his way to Boston and in 1859 organized the famous "Gilmore's
        Band."
    B. During the Civil War he was bandmaster of the Union Army and in 1863
        wrote the popular song, "When Johnny Comes Marching Home."
    C. After the Civil War, Gilmore was stationed in New Orleans where he gave
        many concerts. One concert, in the city square, included 5,000 voices,
        500 bandsmen and a trumpet and drum military corps. "Hail Columbia" was
        sung, accompanied by a battery of cannon firing on each beat of the drums
        and the ringing of church bells in the vicinity.
    D. He staged supercolossal performances, especially at two enormous music
        festivals held in Boston.
        1. The National Peace Jubilee (1869) required an orchestra of 1000 and a
            chorus of 10,000. In addition, there was a powerful organ and
            cannons, bells and 100 firemen pounding anvils during the "Anvil
            Chorus" from Il Trovatore.
        2. The World's Peace Jubilee (1872) was even more stupendous with an or-
            chestra of 2,000 and chorus of 20,000.
            a. Johann Strauss was brought over from Europe for this festival and
                conducted (?) his Blue Danube Waltz with the aid of 100 assistant
                conductors. He described the result as an "unholy row," but they
                all managed to finish together.
```
```

  E. After the Jubilee, Gilmore went to New York and organized a band of 65 players. This concert band toured throughout the United States, Canada and later in Europe (1878).

  F. During the 1880's the band was a summer attraction at Manhattan Beach.

VII. John Philip Sousa (1854-1932)

  A. Born in Washington, D.C., of a Portuguese father and German mother. He studied violin, theory, composition and band instruments. At the age of thirteen he enlisted in the United States Marine Band.

  B. In 1872 he went to Philadelphia to play under Jacques Offenbach during the composer's American tour. He conducted the United States Marine Band from 1880 until 1892. After Gilmore's death in 1892, Sousa formed his own band. This band, which included nineteen of Gilmore's best musicians, became world-famous and was in constant demand, beginning with the Chicago World's Fair in 1893. He made several tours of Europe where he was held in high esteem and received many decorations.

  C. Sousa's published compositions number several hundred, but he is most famous for his marches, which have earned for him the title, "The March King." Many of these marches were inspired by particular events, such as The Washington Post, which was written to celebrate a prize given by the newspaper. Semper Fidelis was adopted as the official march of the Marine Corps.

    1. He also wrote about ten comic operas, a symphonic poem, suites for orchestra, waltzes and songs. He wrote five novels and an autobiography.

  D. Sousa's skill in training musicians had an important influence in the development of band music in America.

    1. Many of the hundreds of musicians who received training in his band became conductors and teachers throughout the country.

      a. A large number of compositions were written by these men and others to fill the needs of the estimated 18,000 bands, amateur and professional, in the United States at the turn of the century.

    2. Giuseppe Creatore and Arthur Pryor were well known band masters in the early part of this century.

  E. Music: M 13-17

VIII. Dudley Buck (1839-1909)

  A. Born in Hartford, Connecticut; studied in Leipzig and Dresden (1858-59) with Hauptmann (composition), Schneider (organ), Moscheles (piano); studied in Paris (1861-62); returned to America (1862) and became organist of Park Church, Hartford; later held church positions in Chicago (St. James), Boston (St. Paul's), Brooklyn (Holy Trinity).

    1. In 1875 Theodore Thomas invited Buck to act as assistant conductor of the Central Park Garden Concerts.

  B. Dudley Buck was a pioneer in the larger fields of choral composition and was one of the first American composers to achieve national recognition.

    1. He had a wide influence on church music through his pupils, some of whom were Shelley, Brewer, Neidlinger and Woodman.

    2. His music was written largely for popular appeal and, although better than much church music of his time, is rarely heard today, except in churches with doubtful musical standards.

    3. Music: M 3, 4

BIBLIOGRAPHY

Books

1. Buck, D.   Illustrations in Choir Accompaniment. New York: G. Schirmer, 1877. (MT 190 B922)

2. Buck, D.   The Influence of the Organ in History. London: W.
        Reeves, 1882. (ML 600 B92)

3. Buck, D.   List of Compositions Published and Unpublished. Manu-
        script, 188-? (ML 95 B922)

4. Ewen, D.   Music Comes to America. New York: Thomas Y. Crowell
        Co., 1942. (ML 200 E94)

5. Gilmore, P. S.   History of the National Peace Jubilee and Great
        Musical Festival, Held in the City of Boston, June, 1869. New York:
        Lee, Shepard, and Dillingham, 1871. (ML 37 B7P35)

6. Gilmore, P. S.   Gilmore's Grand Anniversary Jubilee, 1869-1889.
        Souvenir Porgramme, 1889. (ML 37.7 B7G48)

7. Hall, F. M.   The Story of the Battle Hymn of the Republic. New
        York & London: Harper & Bro., 1916. (ML 3551 H175)

8. Kobbe, G.   Famous American Songs. New York: T. Y. Crowell & Co.,
        1906. (ML 3551 K75)

9. Lewiton, M.   John Philip Sousa, the March King. New York: Didier,
        1944. (ML 3930 S725L67)

10. Mason, W.   Memories of a Musical Life. New York: The Century
        Company, 1901. (ML 417 M412)

11. Root, G. F.   The Musical Curriculum. Chicago: Root & Cady, 1865.
        (MT 7 R782M)

12. Root, G. F.   The Story of a Musical Life. Cincinnati: The J.
        Church Co., 1891. (ML 410 R78)

13. Russell, C. E.   The American Orchestra and Theodore Thomas. New York:
        Doubleday, Page, and Co., 1927. (ML 1211 T4R9)

14. Sonneck, O. G.   Early Opera in America. New York: G. Schirmer, 1915.
        (ML 1711 S699e)

15. Sousa, J. P.   Marching Along. An Autobiography. Boston: Hale,
        Cushman & Flint, 1928. (ML 410 S725m)

16. Upton, W. T.   Anthony Philip Heinrich. New York: Columbia Univer-
        sity Press, 1939. (ML 410 H469U71)

17. Upton, W. T.   William Henry Fry. New York: Thomas Y. Crowell, 1954.

                                Periodicals

1. Damrosch, W.   "Hans von Bülow and the Ninth Symphony," MQ XIII
        (1927), 280.

2. Hill, R. S.   "The Mysterious Chord of Henry Clay Work," Notes (Mar.
        1953), 211.

3. Lowens, I.   "The Triumph of A. P. Heinrich," Musicology I, No. 4
        (1947), 365.

4. Saunders, W.   "The American Opera," ML XIII (1932), 147.

5. Sonneck, O. G.   "Early American Operas," <u>SIM</u> VI (1904-05), 428.

6. Sonneck, O. G.   "Musical Landmarks in New York," <u>MQ</u> VI (1920), 227.

<u>Music</u>

1. Bristow, G. F.   <u>The Cantilena</u>: a collection of songs, duets, trios
    and quartettes.... New York: Abbey and Barrett, 1864.

2. Bristow, G. F.   <u>Rip Van Winkle</u>. New York: G. Schirmer, 1882.
    (M 1503 B861R)

3. Buck, D.   <u>The Coming of the King</u>. Cantata for Advent and
    Christmas-tide. New York: Schirmer, 1895. (M 2023 B92c)

4. Buck, D.   <u>Golden Legend</u>. Scenes from Longfellow's <u>Golden Leg</u>-
        end. A Symphonic Cantata for solos, chorus and orchestra. Cincinnati:
    The John Church Co., 1908. (M 1533 B922g)

5. Fry, W. R.   <u>Selections from Fry's Grand Opera Leonora</u>. Part I.
        Philadelphia: E. Ferrett & Co., 1845. (M 1508 F947L)

6. Heinrich, A. P.   <u>Ein Musikalisches Andenken</u>. Zwei Balladen. Dresden:
        F. G. Ziegra, 1853. (M 1621 H469)

7. Heinrich, A. P.   <u>Two Presentation Volumes</u>. Musical compositions by A.
        P. Heinrich presented to Elizabeth, Empress of Austria. New York: Pub-
        lished by the author, 1853. (M 1.A13 H469)

8. Howard, J. T.   <u>A Program of Early and Mid-nineteenth Century American</u>
        <u>Songs</u>. New York: J. Fischer and Bro., 1931. (M 1629 H849) (<u>EMCS</u>)

9. Mason, W. and E. S. Hoadly. <u>A Method for the Piano-forte</u>. New York: Mason
        Bros., 1867. (MT 222 M412)

10. Mason, W.   <u>Touch and Technique for Artistic Piano Playing</u>. Phil-
        adelphia: Presser, 1889. (MT 225 M41t)

11. <u>Our National War Songs</u>. A complete collection of our grand old war songs,
        battle songs, etc. Cleveland and Chicago: S. Brainard's Sons, 1884.
        (M 1629 B81)

12. Root, G. F.   <u>The Bugle-Call</u>. Chicago: Root & Cady, 1863.
        (M 1639 R782b)

13. Sousa, J. P.   <u>A Collection of Twenty Favorite Marches for Piano</u>.
        New York: C. Fischer, 1890. (M 28 S725)

14. Sousa, J. P.   <u>El Capitan</u>. Comic opera in Three Acts. Cincinnati
        and New York: John Church Co., 1896. (M 1503 S725c)

15. Sousa, J. P.   <u>National, Patriotic and Typical Airs of All Lands</u>.
        New York: C. Fischer, 1890. (M 1627 S725)

16. Sousa, J. P.   <u>The Sousa March Folio</u>. Cincinnati: John Church Co.,
        1902. (M 28 S725sc)

17. Sousa, J. P.   <u>The Stars and Stripes Forever</u>. Facsimile of the
        original manuscript. (M 218 S725s)

18. <u>The Union Song Book</u>. New York: Leavitt and Allen, 186-. (M 1639 L439)

19. Work, B. G.   <u>Songs</u> <u>of</u> <u>Henry</u> <u>Clay</u> <u>Work</u>: <u>Poet</u> <u>and</u> <u>Composer</u> (1832-
       1884).   New York: Press of J. J. Little and Ives Co., 190-?
       (M 1620 W926s)

Records

<u>Composer</u> <u>and</u> <u>Title</u>	<u>Recording</u>	<u>ESM</u> <u>No.</u>
1. Buck, D.		
a. Festival Te Deum in E flat	Vic 31781	R 2091
	Vic 35674	R 1910
b. Rock of Ages	Vic 16269	R 333
2. The Confederacy	Col SL-220	LP 1442
a. General Lee's Grand March		
b. All Quiet Along the Potomac Tonight		
c. The Bonnie Blue Flag		
d. Lorena		
e. The Yellow Rose of Texas		
f. Somebody's Darling		
g. We All Went Down to New Orleans for Bales		
h. General Robert E. Lee's Farewell Order to The Army of Northern Virginia, Appomattox Courthouse, Virginia, April 10, 1865		
i. The Conquered Banner		
j. Dixie's Land with Quickstep and Interlude: Year of Jubilo		
3. Sousa, J. P.	Mer MG-40007	ELP 68
a. Fairest of the Fair		
b. Manhattan Beach		
c. Black Horse Troop		
d. Daughters of Texas		
e. Rifle Regiment		
f. Corcoran Cadets		
g. Hands Across the Sea		
h. Semper Fidelis		
i. Washington Post March	Col A-5535	R 1669
4. Steffe, W.		
a. Battle Hymn of the Republic (1856)	Col M-329	A 599
5. Thompson, H. S.		
a. Lilly Dale (1852)	Col M-329	A 599
6. White, C.		
a. Lubly Fan (1844)	Col M-329	A 599
7. Work, H. C.		
a. Marching through Georgia (1865)	Col M-329	A 599

N.º 31.
THE TOWER OF BABEL
OR LANGUAGE CONFOUNDED.

SINFONIA CANONICALE, or the Symphony of Indefinite Perplexity.(M.S.)
MOST RESPECTFULLY & HUMBLY DEDICATED TO HIS IMPERIAL HIGHNESS.
STEPHAN, Vice Roy of **BOHEMIA**, &c.&c.&c.

N.º 32.
JOHANNISBERG,
OR THE FESTIVAL OF THE VINTAGERS ON THE RHINE.
Grand Divertissement champêtre, pour l'Orchestre.(M.S.) Most respectfully & humbly Dedicated to
HIS SERENE HIGHNESS,
PRINCE GEORGE DE METTERNICH.

N.º 33.
THE ELKHORN PYRAMID, OR
THE INDIANS' OFFERING TO THE SPIRIT OF THE PRAIRIES, *Fantaisie Mystique*.
Pour l'Orchestre.(M.S.) Most respectfully & humbly Dedicated to
HIS SERENE HIGHNESS,
MAXIMILIAN, PRINCE DE WIED, &c.&c.&c.

N.º 34.
TO THE SPIRIT OF BEETHOVEN.
GRANDE SINFONIA caratteristica.(In Manoscritto) Most respectfully & humbly Dedicated to
His Serene Highness,
Prince FERDINAND of LOBKOWITZ, &c.&c.

N.º 35.
THE EMPRESS QUEEN AND THE MAGYARS.
SINFONIA PATRIOTICO-DRAMATICA *Piena Orchestra.(M.S.)* A tribute to the MEMORY OF THE
EMPRESS, MARIA THERESIA, *Designed to portray the following* HISTORICAL INCIDENTS:
THE CONVOCATION OF THE DIET AT PRESBURG on the 11.th of September A.D. 1741.
MARIA THERESIA'S APPEAL AND CHIVALRIC RESPONSE of the HUNGARIAN MAGNATES.
Most respectfully & humbly Dedicated to Her Imperial Majesty.
CAROLINE AUGUSTA, *Empress of Austria, Queen of Hungaria* &c.&c.&c.&c.

N.º 36.
LIKEWISE.
The fair Daughters of the Western World.
Capriccio leggiadro, scherzevole, per Grande Orchestra.

N.º 37.
The War of the Elements & the Thunders of Niagara,
SCENA MAGNIFICA & GRAN CAPRICCIO STREPITOSO. *per Piena Orchestra.(M.S.)* Also:

N.º 38.
THE WASHINGTONIAD OR THE DEEDS OF A HERO.
AN AMERICAN FESTIVE OUVERTURE, *For full Orchestra.(M.S.) Most respectfully & humbly*
DEDICATED TO HIS MAJESTY. **LOUIS PHILIPPE**, KING OF THE FRENCH &c.&c.&c.&c.

N.º 39.
THE DEDICATION WALTZ.
(Printed.)

A page from the <u>Presentazioni Musicali</u> from
Anthony Philip Heinrich's collection of music dedicated
to Empress Elizabeth Amelie Eugenie of Austria

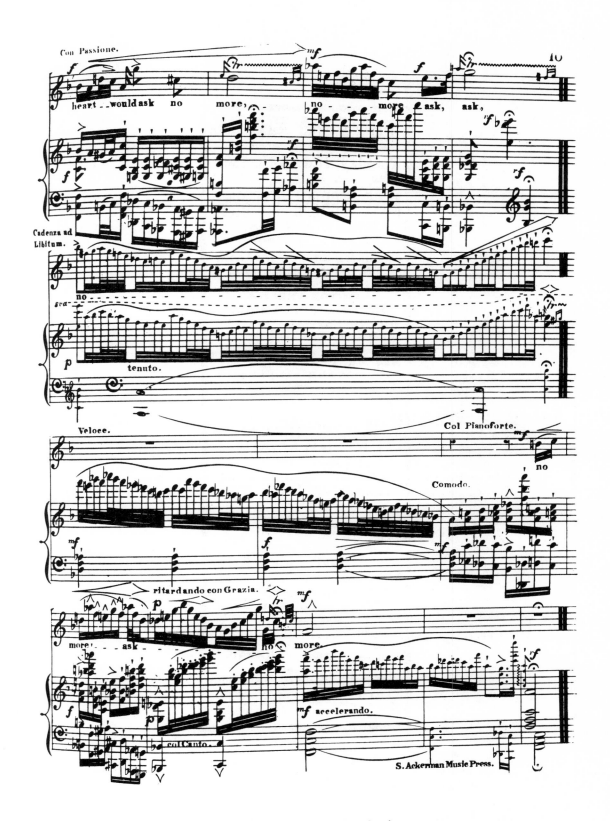

The concluding measures of the song
"Love's Enchantment" by Anthony Philip Heinrich, 1850

Program of the début of Teresa Carreño

THURSDAY AFTERNOON, JUNE 6, 1889,

At 1.30 o'clock.

ORGAN CONCERT — — W. J. D. LEAVITT, ORGANIST.

PROGRAMME.

At 2.30 o'clock.

1. OVERTURE. — "Leonore, No. 3" . . . . *Beethoven*
   GILMORE'S BAND.

2. ARIA FOR TENOR. — From "The Iron Mask" . . . . *A. Thomas*
   HERR DE DANCKWARDT.

3. QUARTETTE FOR FRENCH HORNS. — "Annie Laurie" . . *Dudley Buck*
   From the arrangement for male voices.
   MESSRS. WESTON, CASO, RINGER, AND ZILM.

4. "GLORIA." — From Twelfth Mass . . . . *Mozart*
   **SUNG BY THE RE-UNION CHORUS OF SINGERS FROM NEW ENGLAND
   CHORAL SOCIETIES THAT PARTICIPATED IN THE JUBILEE OF 1869,
   ACCOMPANIED BY THE ORGAN AND GILMORE'S BAND.**

5. RHAPSODIE HONGROISE, No. 12 . . . . *Liszt*
   GILMORE'S BAND.

6. ARIA FOR BASSO. — "She Alone Charmeth my Sadness." . . . . *Gounod*
   MR. WHITNEY.

7. SCOTCH SYMPHONY (Two Movements only) . . . . *Mendelssohn*
   GILMORE'S BAND.

8. CAVATINA FOR SOPRANO. — "Una Voce poco fa" . . . . . . *Rossini*
   MME. STONE-BARTON.

9. MORCEAUX DE SALON. — Valse Caprice . . . . *Rubinstein*
   GILMORE'S BAND.

10. CAVATINA. — "Ah, Quel Giorno" (Semiramide) . . . . *Rossini*
    MISS CAMPBELL.

11. CORNET SOLO (Selected) . . . . *Liberati*
    SIGNOR LIBERATI.

12. POPULAR FANTAISIE. — "Le Carnival de Venise" . . . . *Paganini*
    GILMORE'S BAND.

The following Soloists will each play a variation of his own composition on the
above theme: —

1. EUPHONIUM	. . . .	SIGNOR RAFFAYOLO
2. CLARINET	. . . .	SIGNOR STENGLER
3. FLUGEL HORN	. . . .	HERR RITZE
4. PICCOLO	. . . .	SIGNOR DE CARLO
5. SAXOPHONE	. . . .	MONS. LEFEBRE
6. CORNET	. . . .	MR. B. C. BENT
7. FLUTE	. . . .	MR. JOHN COX
8. ORPHEON	. . . .	MR. HARRY WHITTIER
9. BASSOONS	. . . .	MESSRS RUPP and CAVANAGH
10. OBOE	. . . .	SIGNOR DE CHIARRI
11. CORNET	. . . .	MR. CHAS. PETIT
12. PETIT CLARINET	. . . .	MATUS UR
13. BASS ANTONIOPHONE	. . . .	MR. ELDEN BAKER
14. TROMBONE	. . . .	MR. WILSON
15. BASS CLARINET	. . . .	ERNST WEBER

GILMORE'S BAND.

13. QUARTETTE. — From "Martha" . . . . *Flotow*
    **MME. STONE-BARTON, MISS CAMPBELL, MESSRS. DANCKWARDT
    AND WHITNEY.**

14. NATIONAL AIR. — "Star Spangled Banner" . . . . *Key*
    **SOLO BY MME. BARTON; CHORUS, ORGAN, BAND, AND ARTILLERY
    ACCOMPANIMENT.**

MUSICAL DIRECTOR, P. S. GILMORE.

The STEINWAY PIANO used at all Gilmore Concerts.

A program given in Boston by Gilmore's Band,
commemorating the twentieth anniversary of the Peace Jubilee
of 1869

OUTLINE XII

JOHN KNOWLES PAINE AND THE BOSTON GROUP

John Knowles Paine--The Boston Group
George Chadwick--Arthur Foote--Horatio Parker
Mrs. H. H. A. Beach--Arthur Whiting

I. John Knowles Paine (1839-1906)

A. American music had become thoroughly Germanized by the Germans who set-
    tled in America and the migration of many competent American composers
    to Germany. On their return, these men began to write in the larger
    forms which they had learned abroad and took their place with eminent
    European composers of their time. John Knowles Paine is the first
    American composer of works in larger forms whose music is still heard
    today.

B. Born in Portland, Maine; studied with Kotzschmar and then went to Berlin
    and studied with Haupt (counterpoint) and others (1858-61). He was ap-
    pointed instructor in music at Harvard University (1862) and to the first
    professorship in music in an American University (Harvard, 1875). He re-
    ceived an honorary Master of Arts at Harvard (1869) and a Doctor of Music
    at Yale (1890).

    1. With Paine's appointment to the full professorship at Harvard (1875),
        students were granted credit for the first time for work in a music
        department.

C. His pupils included many musicians who were to become famous in the de-
    velopment of American music.

    1. Arthur Foote, Sumner Salter, Frederick Converse, John Alden Carpenter,
        Edward Burlingame Hill, Blair Fairchild, Daniel Gregory Mason.

D. Paine's compositions include two symphonies, an oratorio, cantatas, sev-
    eral symphonic poems inspired by Shakespeare and the incidental music to
    Sophocles' Oedipus Tyrannus (1881).

    1. He was commissioned by Theodore Thomas to write a Centennial Hymn for
        the Philadelphia Exposition in 1876 and the Columbus March and Hymn
        for the Chicago World's Fair (1893).

    2. He wrote much program music in German romantic style. In his earlier
        works he shows the influence of Schumann and Mendelssohn and later,
        in spite of himself, of Brahms and Wagner.

    3. His music is characterized in general by a strong rhythmic sense, re-
        gular phrases, powerful climaxes, correct harmonic structure, good
        counterpoint and straight-forward melodic lines.

    4. Prelude to Oedipus Tyrannus
        a. Paine composed a prelude, incidental music and postlude to Sophoc-
            les' tragedy, for a performance in the original Greek by students
            of Harvard University (1881).
        b. The Prelude, in C minor, is scored for woodwinds in pairs, four
            horns, two trumpets, three trombones, kettledrums, strings. The
            incidental music includes a male chorus.

BIBLIOGRAPHY

Books

1. Edwards, G. T.   Music and Musicians of Maine. Portland, Me.: The
        Southworth Press, 1928. (ML 200.7 M22E26)

2. Paine, J. K.   Famous Composers and Their Music. 16 vols. Ed. by T.
        Thomas, J. K. Paine, and K. Klauser. Boston: J. B. Millet Co., 1901.
        Vols. I-VI contain historical essays and illustrations. (M 1 F19.3)

3. Paine, J. K.   The History of Music to the Death of Schubert.
        Boston and London: Ginn & Co., 1907. (ML 160 P145)

4. Wilson, G. H.   The Boston Musical Year Book. Vol. I, season of 1883-
        84. Boston: G. H. Ellis, 1884. (ML 200.4 M98)

Periodicals

1. Howe, M. S. DeW.   "John Knowles Paine," MQ XXV (1939), 257.

2. Mathews, J. L.   "Harvard University." Interview with J. K. Paine.
        Music IX (1896), 644.

3. Obituary Notice   "Prof. John Knowles Paine," Mus. Cour. XVIII (1906),
        19, 20.

4. Obituary Notice   "Prof. J. K. Paine," MT XLVII (1906), 395.

Music

1. Azara. (Opera). Leipzig: Breitkopf & Härtel, 1901. (M 1503 P145A)
        (Vault M 1500 P145A)

2. The Birds of Aristophanes, for male chorus, tenor solo and orchestra. Boston:
        Boston Music Co., 1902. (M 1513 P14b)

3. Centennial Hymn, for chorus and orchestra. Boston: Ditson Co., 1930.
        (M 1533 P145c) (Vault ML 96 P145)

4. Freedom, Our Queen, for chorus. New York: H. W. Gray Co., 1902.
        (M 1549 G779)

5. Fuga Giocosa, Op. 41, for piano. Boston: A. P. Schmidt & Co., 1884.
        (M 25 P145f)

6. Im Frühling, Op. 34 (Symphony No. 2 in A). Boston: A. P. Schmidt, 1880.
        (M 1001 P14.2)

7. The Nativity, Op. 39, for chorus, soli, and orchestra. Boston: A. P. Schmidt,
        1903. (M 2045 P145N)

8. Oedipus Tyrannus of Sophocles, for male chorus and orchestra. Boston: A. P.
        Schmidt, 1908. (M 1510 P1450)

9. Overture to As You Like It, Op. 28. Leipzig: Breitkopf & Härtel, 1907.
        (M 1004 P145a)

10. Poseidon und Amphitrite. Symphonic poem. Leipzig: Breitkopf & Härtel, 1907.
        (M 1002 P145P)

11. St. Peter. Oratorio. Boston: Ditson & Co., 1872. (M 2003 P145S)

12. Shakespeare's Tempest. Symphonic poem. Leipzig: Breitkopf & Härtel, 1907.
        (M 1002 P145T)

13. String Quartet in D major, Op. 5. Ms. Film No. 34

14. Symphony No. 1, Op. 23. Leipzig: Breitkopf & Härtel, 1908. (M 1001 P14.1)

<u>Records</u>

<u>Title</u>	<u>Recording</u>	<u>ESM</u> <u>No</u>.
Prelude to <u>Oedipus</u> <u>Tyrannus</u>, Op. 35	Vic M-608	A 1137
	Vic 15658	R 18

II. The Boston Group

    A. This group of musicians -- Chadwick, Foote, Parker, Whiting -- living
        about the same time in Boston, were united by their common musical in-
        terests, personal friendships and background. Mrs. Beach is usually
        included although she was not actually a member of the Boston Group.
        1. They met from time to time for critical consideration of each other's
            works. With the exception of Whiting, they were important teachers
            of theory and composition.
        2. Although their personal style varies, common characteristics of their
            music are strong rhythms, use of classical forms, regularity of phrase
            structure, German romanticism, adherence to academically correct
            harmony and counterpoint.

III. George Whitefield Chadwick (1854-1931)

    A. Born in Lowell, Massachusetts; early studies with Dudley Buck, George
        Whiting and Eugene Thayer in Boston; head of music department at Olivet,
        Michigan (1876). He studied at the Leipzig Conservatory with Reinecke
        and Jadassohn (1877-1878) and composition and organ with Rheinberger at
        Munich (1879).
    B. Chadwick settled in Boston (1880) as organist at the South Congregational
        Church and taught harmony and composition at the New England Conservatory.
        He was appointed Director there in 1893 and became an important figure in
        the field of music education. He received honorary degrees from Yale
        (M.A.) and Tufts College (LL.D).
    C. Among his pupils (some of whom had studied with Paine) were Horatio
        Parker, Arthur Whiting, Sidney Homer, William Grant Still, Frederick
        Converse, Henry Hadley, Daniel Gregory Mason, Arthur Shepherd, Edward
        Burlingame Hill, Paul White.
        1. He has written an important theory text.
    D. His compositions include three symphonies, overtures, symphonic poems,
        string quartets, three operas, large choral works and over 100 published
        songs.
        1. His twenty major works for orchestra include <u>Rip</u> <u>Van</u> <u>Winkle</u> (1879),
            one of six Overtures; <u>Jubilee</u> (1907), from four Symphonic Sketches;
            <u>Tam</u> <u>O'Shanter</u> (1907), a "ballade for orchestra."
        2. His songs include: <u>Allah</u>; <u>Danza</u>; <u>Ballad</u> <u>of</u> <u>Trees</u> <u>and</u> <u>the</u> <u>Master</u>
            (Sidney Lanier).
    E. Chadwick was a sophisticated, yet eclectic composer. His style is
        characterized by rhythmic vitality and freedom, colorful orchestration,
        attractive melodic lines and harmony, and counterpoint that is more
        virile and less sentimental than some others of his group.

BIBLIOGRAPHY

<u>Books</u>

1. Chadwick, G. W.   <u>Commemorative</u> <u>Tribute</u> <u>to</u> <u>Horatio</u> <u>Parker</u>. New York:
      Academy of Arts and Letters, 1922. (ML 410 P23c)

2. Chadwick, G. W.   <u>Harmony,</u> <u>a</u> <u>Course</u> <u>of</u> <u>Study</u>. Boston: B. F. Wood Mus-
      ic Co., 1925. (MT 50 C432.65)

Periodicals

1. Engel, C.   "George W. Chadwick," MQ X (1924), 438.

2. Langley, A. L.   "Chadwick and the New England Conservatory of Music,"
        MQ XXI (1935), 39.

3. Macdougall, H. C.   "George W. Chadwick: An Appreciation of a Disting-
        uished Life," Diapason XXII (May, 1931), 8.

Music

1. Allah. Song for low voice. Boston: A. P. Schmidt, 1887. (M 1620 C43a)

2. A Ballad of Trees and the Master. Sacred song for high voice. Boston:
        Ditson Co., 1899. (M 2110 S123.4)

3. The Danza, Op. 14 (Six songs, no. 1). Boston: A. P. Schmidt Co., 1913.
        (M 1621 C432d)

4. I Know Two Eyes, Op. 14 (Six songs, no. 4). Boston: A. P. Schmidt & Co.,
        1885. (M 1620 C43d)

5. Judith. Lyric drama for soli, chorus and orchestra. New York: G. Schirmer,
        1901. (M 2003 C43J)

6. Noël. A Christmas pastoral for soli, chorus and orchestra. London: Novello
        & Co., Ltd., 1909. (M 2045 C43)

7. Quartet No. 4 in E Minor. New York: Schirmer, 1902. (M 452 C43)

8. Rip Van Winkle. Overture for orchestra. Revised edition. Boston: C. C.
        Birchard & Co., 1930. (M 1004 C432R)

9. Symphonic Sketches. Suite for orchestra. 1. Jubilee; 2. Noël; 3. Hobgoblin;
        4. A vagrom ballad. New York: Schirmer, 1907. (M 1003 C432sy)

10. Symphony No. 2 in B-flat Major, Op. 21. Boston: A. P. Schmidt & Co., 1888.
        (M 1001 C43.2)

11. Symphony No. 3 in F-Major. Boston: A. P. Schmidt, 1896. (M 1001 C43.3)

12. Tam O'Shanter. Symphonic ballade for orchestra. Boston: Boston Music Co.,
        1917. (M 1002 C432T)

Records

Title	Recording	ESM No.
1. Andante Simplice from Quartet in E Minor	Vic M-558 Vic 15417	A 303 R 530
2. Jubilee (No. 1 from Symphonic Sketches)	Vic M-608	A 1137
3. Noël (No. 2 from Symphonic Sketches)	Vic 18274	R 1422

IV. Arthur William Foote (1853-1937)

   A. Born in Salem; studied with Paine at Harvard (M.A., 1875); encouraged by
       Benjamin J. Lang to become a professional musician; organist at First
       Unitarian Church, Boston (1878-1910). Foote was one of the founders of

the American Guild of Organists (1896). He taught at the New England
Conservatory and privately, and performed professionally as a concert
pianist.
    1. Foote was one of the few important composers of his time who did not
        go to Europe to study.
B. His compositions include eight works for full or string orchestra (no
    symphonies), many works for chorus a cappella and with orchestra, pieces
    for organ and piano, 125 songs, four string quartets, two piano quartets,
    a piano quintet, a concerto for cello (1894).
    1. He has written important theory texts.
C. Foote's style is highly refined and is basically harmonic; earlier works
    show the influence of Brahms. His music is melodically and rhythmically
    interesting, and he makes some use of modes and, in choral music, the
    leitmotif.
    1. Suite for Strings in E (1907-8)
        a. Prelude--Pizzicato--Fugue
        b. The Prelude, in E major, is based entirely on the first phrase of
           eight notes with much use of imitation.
        c. The Pizzicato, in A minor, is interrupted by an Adagietto, in F
           major, played arco with strings muted.
        d. The Fugue, in E minor, is thoroughly worked out, but without the
           use of augmentation, inversion, etc. The first four notes of the
           theme are heard often by themselves and a long pedal point appears
           at the last return of the theme.
    2. Night Piece for flute and strings (1911-14)

BIBLIOGRAPHY

Books

1. Foote, A. W.   An Autobiography. Norwood, Mass.: Privately printed
      at the Plimpton Press, 1946. (ML 410 F688)

2. Foote, A. W.   A Key to the Exercises in Modern Harmony. Boston: A.
      P. Schmidt Co., 1936. (MT 50 F688K)

3. Foote, A. W.   Modern Harmony. Boston: A. P. Schmidt, 1905.
      (MT 50 F68)

4. Foote, A. W.   Modulation and Related Harmonic Questions. Boston:
      A. P. Schmidt Co., 1919. (MT 52 F68)

5. Foote, A. W.   Some Practical Things in Piano Playing. Boston: A. P.
      Schmidt, 1909. (MT 200 F68s)

Periodicals

1. Foote, A. W.   "A Bostonian Remembers," MQ XXIII (1937), 37.

2. Foote, A. W.   "The Relation of Consonance to Dissonance," Etude LV
      (1937), 504.

3. Foote, A. W.   "Rhythm and Accent," Etude LI (1933), 653.

4. Jacobi, F.   "Homage to Arthur Foote," MM XIV (1937), 198.

5. Macdougall, H. C.   "Arthur Foote's Life Comes to Its Close," Diapason
      XXVIII (1937), 3.

Music

1. Francesca da Rimini, Op. 24. Symphonic prologue. Boston: A. P. Schmidt,
   1892. (M 1004 F68s)

2. I'm Wearing Awa' to the Land o' the Leal. Boston: A. P. Schmidt Co.
   (M 1621 F688I)

3. O Swallow, Swallow Flying South. Boston: A. P. Schmidt, 1896.
   (M 1621 F688Os)

4. Quintet, for piano and strings in A minor, Op. 38. Leipzig: Schmidt, 1898.
   (M 512 F68)

5. Sonata in G Minor, for violin and piano. Boston: A. P. Schmidt, 1890.
   (M 219 F688)

6. Suite in D, for organ, Op. 54. Boston: Schmidt, 1904. (M 7 F68)

7. Suite in E Major, for string orchestra, Op. 63. Boston: Schmidt, 1909.
   (M 1103 F68S)

8. Trio in B Major, for piano, violin and violoncello, Op. 65. Boston: Schmidt,
   1909. (M 312 F688.2)

Records

Title	Recording	ESM No.
1. A Night Piece (flute and string quartet)	Col 70339	R 681
	Dec 4013	LP 1443
2. Suite for Strings in E, Op. 63	Vic DM-962	A 82
		A 1405
	Mer 40001	ELP 62

V. Horatio William Parker (1863-1919)

   A. Born in Auburndale, Massachusetts; began the study of music at fourteen;
      became a church organist at sixteen and was one of Chadwick's first
      pupils in composition. He studied at the Royal School of Music in
      Munich with Rheinberger and perfected his contrapuntal style (1882). He
      returned to New York and taught at the Cathedral School in Garden City
      and National Conservatory in New York (where Dvorak was director). He
      became organist in New York (Holy Trinity) and in 1893 in Boston (Trinity
      Church). He conducted choral societies in several cities and became head
      of the music department at Yale University. He was awarded a Doctor of
      Music degree by Cambridge University, England (1892).
   B. Parker's compositions include 40 choral works, two operas (Mona; Fairy-
      land), nine orchestral works, an organ concerto, pieces for voice, piano,
      organ and chamber ensembles.
   C. His students included Douglas Moore, Quincy Porter, Charles Ives, Edward
      Shippen Barnes, Seth Bingham.
   D. Parker's style is facile, but somewhat uneven in quality. He is most
      successful in choral music, but his harmony and counterpoint are inclined
      to be academic and sometimes commonplace.
      1. Hora Novissima (1891-92) (Day of Judgment)
         a. One of Parker's outstanding works, it has been widely performed.
            Since 1897 over 178 performances have been given with full orches-
            tra and many more with piano and organ. In 1899 it was performed
            at the Three Choirs Festival in Worcester, England, the first

American composition to be heard there.
b. The text was translated by Parker's mother from the twelfth century Latin hymn of Barnard de Morlaix, a monk in the Abbey of Cluny, France.
c. The work contains some vigorous, effective writing with skillful handling of massed effects, fugal style, texture and hymn-like themes.
d. "Pars mea" shows skillful contrapuntal writing and "Spe modo vivetur" reveals Parker's sensitivity to the text with its use of three-four, four-four, five-four, two-four and three-two time.
  2. Mona (1912)
a. Won a $10,000 prize offered by the Metropolitan Opera House. His opera Fairyland (1915) also won a $10,000 prize offered by the National Federation of Music Clubs. The librettos of both operas were by Brian Hooker, professor of English at Yale. Mona was never revived after the first season at the Metropolitan (1912). The story deals with Mona, princess of Britain during the Roman invasion, who is torn between her love for the son of the Roman governor and hatred of the Roman conquerors.

BIBLIOGRAPHY

Books

1. Chadwick, G. W.   Commemorative Tribute to Horatio Parker. New York: Academy of Arts and Letters, 1922. (ML 410 P23c)

2. Rosenfeld, P.   Musical Chronicle (1917-1923) (H. Parker's Mona). New York: Harcourt, Brace & Co., 1923. (ML 60 R813M)

3. Semler, I.   Horatio Parker. A memoir for his grandchildren. New York: G. P. Putnam's Sons, 1942. (ML 410 P239S47)

Periodicals

1. Rosenfeld, P.   "One of Our Parents" (Horatio Parker), MM XIX (1942), 215.

2. Smith, D. S.   "A Study of Horatio Parker," MQ XVI (1930), 153.

Music

1. Concerto, for organ and orchestra, Op. 55. (Arrangement for organ solo by D. S. Smith). London: Novello & Co., 1903. (M 13 P23S)

2. Dream-King and His Love, Op. 31, for chorus, tenor solo and orchestra. New York: G. Schirmer, 1893. (M 1533 P23D)

3. Fairyland. Opera. New York: Schirmer, 1914. (M 1503 P23f)

4. Hora Novissima, for soli, chorus and orchestra. London: Novello & Co., 1893. (M 2003 P23h)

5. The Legend of St. Christopher, for soli, chorus, orchestra and organ. London: Novello, Ewer & Co., 1898. (M 2003 P23L)

6. Mona. Opera. New York: Schirmer, 1911. (M 1503 P23M)

7. A Star Song, for solo, quartet, chorus and orchestra. Cincinnati: John Church Co., 1902. (M 1530 P239s)

8. <u>Suite</u>, for piano, violin and violoncello. Op. 35. New York: Schirmer, 1904.
       (M 312 P23)

9. <u>A Wanderer's Psalm</u>, Op. 50, for soli, chorus and orchestra. London: Novello
       & Co., 1900(?) (M 2023 P23w)

Record

<u>Title</u>	<u>Recording</u>	<u>ESM</u> <u>No</u>.
<u>Hora Novissima</u>	ARS	LP

VI. Arthur Battelle Whiting (1861-1936)

   A. Born in Cambridge, Massachusetts; studied at the New England Conservatory with Sherwood, Maas and Chadwick; studied at the Munich Conservatory with Rheinberger and others (1883-85); lived in Boston until 1895; settled in New York; gave educational chamber-music concerts at eastern universities (after 1907); gave concerts of early music with Edson (violin), Barrère (flute), Kefer (viola da gamba), himself at the harpsichord.

     1. He is the nephew of George E. Whiting (1842-1923), composer and organist. George Whiting studied with Best in Liverpool (1863), Haupt in Berlin (1874); taught at New England Conservatory (until 1879), Cincinnati College of Music (1879-82), New England Conservatory (1883-97); organist in several churches.

   B. His compositions, comparatively few in number, include a <u>Concert Overture</u>, <u>Fantasy</u> for piano and orchestra, <u>Suite</u> for horns and strings, incidental music for <u>The Golden Cage</u> (a dance pageant), a string quartet, pieces for piano and songs.

BIBLIOGRAPHY

<u>Book</u>

1. Whiting, A.   <u>Pianoforte Pedal Studies</u>. New York: G. Schirmer, Inc., 1932. (MT 227 W597)

<u>Periodicals</u>

1. Mason, D. G.   "Arthur Whiting," <u>MQ</u> XXIII (1937), 26.

2. Whiting, A.   "The Lesson of the Clavichord," <u>New Music Review</u> VIII (Jan., 1909), 69.

<u>Music</u>

1. <u>Fantasy</u>, for piano and orchestra, Op. 11. New York: Schirmer, 1897.
       (M 215 S598)

2. <u>Floriana</u>, for solo voices and piano. New York: G. Schirmer, L1901.
       (M 1558 W598F)

3. <u>The Golden Cage</u>, for small orchestra. New York: G. Schirmer, 1926.
       (M 1520 W59)

4. <u>Suite Moderne</u>, Op. 15, for piano. New York: Schirmer, 1900. (M 21 R29A)

VI. Mrs. H. H. A. Beach (Amy Marcy Cheney) (1867-1944)

    A. Born in Henniker, New York; early studies with teachers in Boston; largely self-taught in counterpoint and composition. She made her debut as a pianist in Boston in the Moscheles <u>Concerto in G Minor</u> (1883). She toured Europe with great success and introduced her own compositions in Hamburg, Leipzig and Berlin (1911-1915). On her return to America, she devoted herself to composition and some concert work.

    B. Her compositions include a piano concerto, symphony (<u>Gaelic</u>), piano quintet, sonata for violin and piano, suite for two pianos (1932), a string quartet (1929), songs and music for the church.

        1. Her best known songs are: <u>The Year's at the Spring</u>; <u>Ah, Love but a Day</u>; <u>Ecstasy</u>.

        2. Important choral works include <u>Benedictus es Domini</u> (1924); <u>Canticle of the Sun</u> (1928); <u>Christ in the Universe</u> (1931).

BIBLIOGRAPHY

<u>Book</u>

1. Goetschius, P.   <u>Mrs. H. H. A. Beach</u>. Analytical sketch. Boston: A. P. Schmidt, 1906. (ML 410 B365G59)

<u>Periodicals</u>

1. Adams, C.   "The American Genius of World Renown: Mrs. H. H. A. Beach," <u>Etude</u> XLVI (1928), 34.

2. Anonymous   "Mrs. H. H. A. Beach Honored," <u>Musical Leader</u> LXXII (May 25, 1940), 9.

3. Beach, H. H. A.   "Emotion Versus Intellect in Music," <u>MTNA</u> XXVI (1931), 17.

4. Beach, H. H. A.   "Twenty-Fifth Anniversary of a Vision," <u>MTNA</u> XXVII (1932), 45.

5. Tuthill, B. C.   "Mrs. H. H. A. Beach," <u>MQ</u> XXVI (1940), 297.

<u>Music</u>

1. <u>Ah, Love But a Day!</u> (Browning songs, no. 2). Boston: A. P. Schmidt, 1900. (M 1621 B365a)

2. <u>The Canticle of the Sun</u>, Op. 123, for soli, chorus and orchestra. Boston: A. P. Schmidt, 1928. (M 2023 B365c)

3. <u>Ecstasy</u>. (Song album no. 1). Boston: A. P. Schmidt, 1891. (M 1621 B365s)

4. <u>Five Improvisations</u>, for piano. Boston: A. P. Schmidt.

5. <u>Quintet in F-sharp Minor</u>, Op. 67, for piano, 2 violins, viola and violoncello. Boston: Schmidt, 1909. (M 512 B36)

6. <u>Suite</u>, for two pianos, four hands. Cincinnati: J. Church Co., 1924. (M 214 B36)

7. <u>Symphony (Gaelic) in E Minor</u>, Op. 32. Leipzig: A. P. Schmidt, 1897. (M 1001 B36)

8. <u>Theme and Variations</u>, for flute and string quartet, Op. 80. New York:

Schirmer, 1920. (M 562 B365)

9. The Year's at the Spring. Song. Boston: A. P. Schmidt, 1928.
      (M 1621 B365y)

Record

Title	Recording	ESM No.
Improvisation No. 2 (from Five Improvisa-tions	Vic M-764	A 939 A 1435

OUTLINE XIII

CONTEMPORARIES OF THE BOSTON GROUP

Ethelbert W. Nevin--Henry F. Gilbert--Edward MacDowell

I. Ethelbert Woodbridge Nevin (1862-1901)

    A. Life
        1. Born in Vineacre, near Pittsburgh, Pennsylvania; went to Europe in 1877 and studied piano in Dresden; returned to Pittsburgh a year later; went to Boston in 1881 to study with B. J. Lang (1837-1909) and S. A. Emery (1841-1891). He settled in Pittsburgh as pianist and teacher in 1883, but returned to Europe in 1884 and studied with Klindworth and Von Bülow.
        2. In 1886 he returned to America and made his debut as a pianist in Pittsburgh. He lived in Boston and New York and in 1891 returned to Europe for six years. His later years were marked by a nervous disorder and ill health, and he died at the age of 38.
    B. Music
        1. Nevin's works consist chiefly of short piano pieces and songs, which reveal his lyric gift. They are, however, mostly of the sentimental, salon type. The Sketch Book, Op. 2 (1888), a collection of songs and piano pieces, brought his music before the public and met with immediate success.
        2. Well-known songs include "The Rosary (1898), "Mighty Lak' a Rose" (1901).
        3. Water Scenes (1891), which includes one of his most popular pieces, Narcissus, and A Day in Venice (1896), written while he was in Venice, are his best known suites for piano.

BIBLIOGRAPHY

Books

1. Howard, J. T.   Ethelbert Nevin. New York: T. Y. Crowell Co., 1935.
    (ML 410 N526H84)

2. Thompson, V.   The Life of Ethelbert Nevin. Boston: The Boston
    Music Co., 1913. (ML 410 N526Y47)

Periodical

1. Rogers, F.   "Some Memories of Ethelbert Nevin," MQ III (1917),358.

Music

1. Album of Favorite Songs. New York: J. Church, 1899. (M 1620 N526a)

2. A Day in Venice. Cincinnati: J. Church Co., 1898. (M 25 N526g)

3. The Rosary. Boston: Boston Music Co., 1900. (M 1621 N526r.2)

4. Sketchbook, Op. 2. Boston: Boston Music Co., 1888. (M 1621 N526s)

5. Twenty-Six Favorite Compositions, for voice and piano. Boston: Boston Music Co., 1943. (M 1621 N526c)

6. Water Scenes. Suite for piano. Boston: Boston Music Co., 1891. (M 25 N526w)

Records

Title	Recording	ESM No.
1. Mighty Lak' a Rose (Farrar & Kreisler)	Vic 89108	R 2049
(Nordica)	Col 30486	R 900
(Alda)	Vic 64308	R 2175
2. Narcissus (Pryor's Band)	Vic 16029	R 1827
3. The Rosary (Schumann-Heink)	Vic 88108	R 2184
(Kreisler)	Vic 64502	R 362

II. Henry F. Gilbert (1868-1928)

  A. Life
    1. Born in Somerville, Massachusetts; studied violin at the New England Conservatory; became MacDowell's first American pupil (Boston, 1889-92). He entered business, composing when he had the opportunity. In 1895 he made his first trip to Paris.
    2. He returned to Paris in 1901 to hear Charpentier's Louise and was so impressed that he decided to devote himself entirely to composition.
  B. Music
    1. Gilbert became associated with Arthur Farwell (1902) and began to employ Negro tunes and rhythms extensively in his compositions.
      a. Comedy Overture on Negro Themes (1905)
        1) Originally intended as a prelude to an opera based on the Uncle Remus stories of Joel Harris. A performance by the Boston Symphony Orchestra in 1911 brought Gilbert into prominence.
      b. Dance in the Place Congo (1906)
        1) A rhapsodic poem, later arranged for ballet and produced at the Metropolitan Opera House in 1918.
        2) The music is based on fragments of creole songs and dances as they might have been used by the slaves in the old Place Congo in New Orleans.
        3) The work begins with semi-barbaric rhythms and a note of tragedy; the middle section is largely given over to the frenzied Bamboula, the principal dance of the slaves; the nine-o'clock bell is heard calling the slaves to quarters, and the music gradually grows more serious; after a final cry of revolt against slavery the composition ends in the mood of the beginning.
  C. American folk music
    1. The music of the American Indians and Negroes and the folk music of mountaineers and cowboys, lumberjacks, sailors and others has had a considerable influence on a number of American composers. One of the first to develop an interest in American folk music was the Bohemian composer Dvorak, who was in America from 1892 to 1895.
    2. Composers who have drawn on this music, in addition to Henry F. Gilbert, are Arthur Farwell (1872-1952); Charles Wakefield Cadman (1881-1946), whose Indian opera Shanewis was produced at the Metropolitan (1918); Charles S. Skilton (1868-1941); Frederick Jacobi (1891-1952), Indian Dances (1928); Nathaniel Dett (1882-1943) and William Grant Still (1895-), both Negro composers; David Guion (1895-); John Powell (1882-).

BIBLIOGRAPHY

Books

1. Gilbert, Mrs. H. F.   Comment and Criticism on the Works of Henry F. Gil-

bert. Cambridge, Mass., 1928. (ML 410 G4G4)

2. Fraser, V. L.   The Style of Henry F. Gilbert. ESM Thesis, 1942.

Periodicals

1. Cable, G.   "The Dance in the Place Congo," The Century Magazine
        XXXI (1886), 517.

2. Downes, O.   "An American Composer (Henry F. Gilbert)," MQ IV
        (1918), 23.

3. Gilbert, H. F.   "The American Composer," MQ I (1915), 169.

4. Gilbert, H. F.   "Originality," MQ V (1919), 1.

Music

1. Gilbert, H. F.   Comedy Overture on Negro Themes. New York: H. W.
        Gray, 1912. (M 1004 G464c)

2. Gilbert, H. F.   Dance in the Place Congo. New York: H. W. Gray, 1922.
        (M 1002 G464d)

Records

Composer and Title	Recording	ESM No.
1. Cadman, C. W.		
a. At Dawning (Orchestra)	Vic 45170	R 354
b. From the Land of the Sky-Blue Water		
(Gluck)	Vic 64190	R 1799
(Kreisler)	Vic 1115	R 1718
c. Omaha Indian Tribal Song	Col 30486	R 900
2. Farwell, A.		
a. Navajo War Dance, Op. 20, No. 1 (Behrend)	Vic M-764	A 1435
b. Sourwood Mountain, Op. 78, No. 3	Vic M-764	A 1435
3. Gilbert, H. F.		
a. Dance in the Place Congo (Janssen)	Art 100-A	LP 1
b. Pirate Song (Bispham)	Col A-5778	R 1897

III. Edward MacDowell (1861-1908)

   A. Life
     1. Born in New York; pupil of Teresa Carreño in piano; studied at the
       Paris Conservatory (1876) where he was a classmate of Debussy; en-
       tered the Conservatory at Frankfort, Germany, in 1879 and studied
       with Raff; taught piano at the Darmstadt Conservatory; played his
       first Piano Concerto for Liszt at Weimar (1882); returned to
       Waterford, Connecticut, in 1884 to marry Marian Nevins who had been
       a pupil of his in Germany. He returned to Germany, but in 1888 made
       Boston his home, composing and playing piano recitals.
     2. In 1896 he became head of the new department of music at Columbia
       University, a distinction due to "the greatest musical genius America
       has produced." He now devoted himself entirely to teaching and com-
       position, writing many of his finest works. In 1902 his health began
       to fail, and he resigned his position in 1904. His malady ended in

insanity in 1905.
3. Shortly after his death the MacDowell Memorial Association was formed, and the MacDowell Colony for American composers was established at his summer residence at Peterborough, New Hampshire.
B. Music
1. Due largely to the efforts of Teresa Carreño, who played his piano music in Europe and America, MacDowell achieved fame and recognition in his lifetime.
2. MacDowell's music has a bold harmonic and noble melodic style of marked individuality. His themes are generally short and remarkably expressive, and his rhythms have variety and strength. His works are well proportioned, and he is able to maintain a basic mood throughout a composition.
3. His more important works include the second Indian Suite (1892), his last work for orchestra and an important landmark in American music; the second Piano Concerto (D Minor, Op. 23, 1885); four piano sonatas: Tragica (1893), Eroica (1895), Norse (1900), Keltic (1901).
4. There are many short piano pieces and songs in poetic vein.

BIBLIOGRAPHY

Books

1. Gilman, L.   Edward MacDowell. London & New York: Lane Co., 1906.
        (ML 410 M13G4)

2. Hier, E. G.   The Boyhood and Youth of E. A. MacDowell. Peter-
        borough, N.H.: Nubanusit Press, 1926. (ML 49 M13H6)

3. Lien, B.   An Analytical Study of Selected Piano Works by Edward
        MacDowell. ESM Thesis, 1940.

4. MacDowell, E.   Critical and Historical Essays. Boston & New York:
        A. P. Schmidt, 1912. (ML 60 M13)

5. MacDowell, M. G.   Random Notes on Edward MacDowell and his Music. Bos-
        ton: A. P. Schmidt, 1950. (ML 410 M12M34)

6. Page, E. F.   Edward MacDowell. New York: Dodge Publishing Co.,
        1910. (ML 410 M13P13)

7. Porte, J. F.   Edward MacDowell. London: K. Paul, Trench, Trubner,
        1922. (ML 410 M13P84)

Periodicals

1. Brown, R. W.   "A Listener to the Winds (MacDowell)," MA (Feb. 25,
        1929), 15.

2. Currier, T. P.   "Edward MacDowell as I Knew Him," MQ I (1915), 17.

3. Erskine, J.   "MacDowell at Columbia," MQ XXVIII (1942), 395.

4. Gilman, L.   "Orchestral Master Works (MacDowell's Suite No. 2),"
        MA (Feb. 25, 1929), 17.

5. MacDowell, M.   "MacDowell's 'Peterborough Idea'," MQ XVIII (1932),
        33.

6. McWhood, L.   "Edward MacDowell at Columbia University," MTNAPro
        (1923).

7. Putnam, N. A.   "Ten Ideas Gained from Study with Edward MacDowell,"
        Etude XLVIII (March, 1930), 163.

8. Sinclair, U.   "Memories of Edward MacDowell," Sackbut (Dec., 1925),
        127.

9. Sinclair, U.   "Recollections of Edward MacDowell," Etude LXVI (July,
        1948), 418.

Music

1. Concerto No. 1, Op. 15, for piano and orchestra. Leipzig: Breitkopf &
        Härtel, 1911. (M 1010 M138.1)

2. Concerto No. 2, for piano and orchestra. Op. 23. Leipzig: Breitkopf &
        Härtel, 1907. (M 1010 M138.2)

3. Twelve Etudes. Boston: Boston Music Co., 1950. (M 32 M138)

4. Fireside Tales, Op. 61, for piano. Boston: A. P. Schmidt Co., 1930.
        (M 25 M138f)

5. Forest Idyls, Op. 19, for piano. Leipzig: C. F. Kahnt, 1912. (M 25 M138wa.2)

6. From an Old Garden, Op. 26. Six songs for voice and piano. New York: G.
        Schirmer, 1897. (M 1621 M138f)

7. Six Idyls, for piano. Boston: A. P. Schmidt Co., 1929. (M 25 M1381.2)

8. Six Love Songs, Op. 40. Boston: A. P. Schmidt, 1890. (M 1621 M138s)

9. Marionettes, Op. 38, for piano. Boston: A. P. Schmidt Co., 1929. (M 25 M138m)
        (M 25 M138m)

10. New England Idyls, Op. 62, for piano. Boston: A. P. Schmidt Co., 1902.
        (M 25 M138N)

11. Scotch Poem, Op. 31, No. 2, for piano. Boston: A. P. Schmidt, 1895.
        (M 25 M138pS)

12. Rigaudon, Op. 49, No. 2, for piano. Boston: A. P. Schmidt, 1894.
        (M 25 M138R)

13. Sea Pieces, Op. 55. Boston: A. P. Schmidt, 1926. (M 25 M138s)

14. Sonata No. 1, Op. 45 (Sonata Tragica), for piano. Leipzig: Breitkopf &
        Härtel, 1893. (M 22 M13)

15. Sonata No. 2, Op. 50 (Sonata Eroica), for piano. Leipzig: Breitkopf &
        Härtel, 1895. (M 22 M13)

16. Sonata No. 3, Op. 57 (Norse), for piano. Boston: A. P. Schmidt, 1900.
        (M 22 M13)

17. Sonata No. 4, Op. 59 (Keltic), for piano. Boston: A. P. Schmidt, 1901.
        (M 22 M13)

18. Second Suite (Indian), Op. 48. Leipzig: Breitkopf & Härtel, 1897.
        (M 1003) M131.2)

19. Woodland Sketches, Op. 51. Boston: A. P. Schmidt Co., 1924. (M 25 M138w)

Records

Title	Recording	ESM No.
1. Concerto No. 1 for Piano in A minor, Op. 15 (Rivkin)	West 5190	LP 896
2. Concerto No. 2 for Piano in D Minor, Op. 23 (Sanroma)	Vic M-324	A 373
(Rivkin)	West 5190	LP 896
(Sanroma)	Col ML-4638	ELP 20
3. Fireside Tales, Op. 61 a. Of Br'er Rabbit (Ganz)	Dec A-599	A 1215
4. Improvisation, Op. 46, No. 4 (Ganz)	Dec A-599	A 1215
5. Indian Suite No. 2, Op. 48 (Barlow)	Col MM-373	A 1214
(Dixon)	ARS 3	LP 809

a. Legend
   b. Love Song
   c. In Wartime
   d. Dirge
   e. Village Festival
	Vic 15657	R 17, A 1137

6. March Wind (Virtuoso Studies Nos. 10 & 12, Op. 46) (Behrend)	Vic M-764	A 1435
(Ganz)	Dec A-599	A 1215
7. Marionettes Suite, Op. 38 (Ganz)	Dec A-576	A 1205
8. Of a Tailor and a Bear (Orchestra)	Vic 18598	R 2020

9. Piano Music (J. Kirkpatrick)
   a. Woodland Sketches, Op. 51
   b. Sea Pieces, Op. 55
   c. Fireside Tales, Op. 61
   d. New England Idyls, Op. 62
	Col ML 54372	LP 328

10. Rigaudon, Op. 49, No. 2 (Ganz)	Dec A-599	A 1215
11. Sea Pieces, Op. 55 a. A. D. 1620 (Hess)	Col DB-1235	A 666
(Ganz)	Dec A-599	A 1215
12. Scotch Poem, Op. 31, No. 2 (Ganz)	Dec A-599	A 1215
13. Thy Beaming Eyes (Eddy)	Vic 4368	R 1458
14. To a Wild Rose (Casals)	Col 80817	R 320
(Ganz)	Dec A-599	A 1215
(Celesta)	Vic 17691	R 1681
15. To a Water Lily (Ganz)	Dec A-599	A 1215
16. Witches Dance, Op. 17, No. 2	Clas 1026	LP 1169
17. Woodland Sketches, Op. 51 a. From an Indian Lodge (Sousa's Band)	Vic 17035	R 1660

CHARLES MARTIN LOEFFLER--CHARLES TOMLINSON GRIFFES
DANIEL GREGORY MASON

I. Charles Martin Loeffler (1861-1935)

    A. Life
       1. Born in Alsace; boyhood spent in Russia, Hungary, Switzerland; studied violin in Berlin with Joseph Joachim, composition in Paris with Ernest Guiraud. He came to New York in 1881 and played with Walter Damrosch amd Theodore Thomas. He was a violinist in the Boston Symphony Orchestra (1882-1903), appearing as soloist. He became an American citizen at the age of 26. After 1903 he lived in Boston, teaching and composition. He was the recipient of many honors, including the Doctor of Music from Yale University (1926).
       2. Style
          a. Loeffler's style is highly refined and personal, although colored by French impressionism. He does not make use of "American" idioms, except in Clowns and the Partita for violin and piano, which show some jazz influence. In his later works he uses frequent alternations of duple and triple meter.
          b. The inspiration for much of his music comes from poems, dramas, and texts from classic and modern sources.
          c. Gregorian chant is a strong influence in his mature style. Canticum fratris solis (1925), a setting for solo voice and chamber orchestra of the Canticle of the Sun by St. Francis, uses the liturgical themes "Deo gratias" (LU 53), "Kyrie" (LU 80) and the Easter Introit "Resurrexi" (LU 778). The songs also make use of modal melodies and are generally impressionistic with a spirit of mysticism touched with melancholy.
       3. Music
          a. Loeffler's compositions include works for orchestra, often with a solo instrument, chorus with orchestra and a cappella, chamber music and songs.
          b. The Pagan Poem (1907)
             1) Loeffler's best-known work. It was first conceived as a piece of chamber music (1901), then arranged for two pianos and three trumpets (1903), and finally for symphony orchestra with piano. The Boston Symphony Orchestra gave the first performance in 1907.
             2) It is based on the eighth Eclogue of Virgil in which a Thessalian maiden tries, with the aid of sorcery, to win back her truant lover. The three obbligato trumpets, representing the call of the sorceress, are first heard off-stage and gradually come nearer until they join the orchestra in the maiden's triumph.
          c. Music for Four Stringed Instruments (1923)
             1) The work is in three movements and is dedicated to the memory of an American aviator who lost his life in World War I.
             2) The beginning of the Easter Introit "Resurrexi" (LU 778) appears in plain song notation at the head of the score. This motive forms the principal material of the quartet.
             3) The second movement bears the title "Le Saint Jour de Paques" (Easter Sunday). The fourth string of the cello is tuned down to A where it states the plainsong theme.
             4) The third movement has many changes in tempo, one of which is marked "Tempo di Marcia."
          d. String Quintet in F major (1894)
             1) A one-movement work, scored for the unusual combination of three violins, viola and cello.

2) There are three sections to the work; the second section begins (score, p. 18) with a recitative for viola and has a scherzo-like character with a development of earlier material.
3) The third section (score, p. 29) is a shortened and varied recapitulation of the first section.

BIBLIOGRAPHY

Books

1. Aldrich, R.   Concert Life in New York, 1902-1923. New York: Putnam and Co., 1941. (ML 200.8 N5A36)

2. Boston Symphony Orchestra Programmes, 1921-22, pp. 1124-1132; 1935-36, pp. 168, 177, 182; 1938-39, p. 230 (Loeffler).

3. Gearhart, E.   The Songs of Charles Martin Loeffler. ESM Thesis, 1942.

4. Gilman, L.   Nature in Music and Other Studies in the Tone-Poetry of Today. New York: John Lane Co., 1914. (ML 60 G48n)

5. Norman, G.   Letters of Composers. New York: Alfred Knopf & Shrifts, Marion Co., 1946. (ML 90 N842)

6. Smith, E. E.   A Study of Canticum Fratris Solis by Charles Martin Leeffler. ESM Thesis, 1947.

7. Townsend, R. C.   Technics Used by Charles M. Loeffler in Music for Four Instruments. ESM Thesis, 1948.

Periodicals

1. Engel, C.   "Charles Martin Loeffler," MQ XI (1925), 311.

2. Engel, C.   "Views and Reviews (Charles M. Loeffler)", MQ XXI (1935), 368.

3. Ewen, D.   "Charles M. Loeffler," Chesterian (July-August, 1935), 149.

4. Hill, E. B.   "Charles Martin Loeffler," MM XIII (1935), 26.

5. Tuthill, B. C.   "50 Years of Chamber Music in the U.S.," MTNAPro XXIII (1928), 163.

6. Waters, E. N.   "New Loeffleriana," Library of Congress Quarterly Journal (April-June, 1944), 6.

Music

1. Beat! Beat! Drums! (Walt Whitman) for men's voices. Boston: C. C. Birchard, 1932. (M 1567 L825b)

2. Canticum Fratris Solis for soprano voice and orchestra. Medfield, Mass.: Ms. facsimile, 192-? (M 2.8 L825c). Score (M 1613.3 L825)

3. Deux Rapsodies, Op. 5, pour hautbois, alto et piano. New York: Schirmer, 1905. (M 322 L82)

4. For One Who Fell in Battle. Eight-part chorus for mixed voices a cappella.

New York: G. Schirmer, 1911. (M 1567 L825)

5. Five Irish Fantasies for voice and orchestra. New York: G. Schirmer, 1935.
      (M 1613 L825Im)

6. Four Poems, Op. 15, for voice and piano. New York: G. Schirmer, 1906.
      (M 1621 L825p)

7. Memories of My Childhood. Poem for orchestra. New York: G. Schirmer, 1925.
      (M 1002 L825m)

8. Music for Four Stringed Instruments. New York: G. Schirmer, 1923. Score
      (M 452 L82s); Parts (M 452 L82)

9. A Pagan Poem. New York: G. Schirmer, 1909. (M 1002 L825p). Arrangement
      for two pianos (M 215 L825p)

10. Partita for violin and piano. New York: G. Schirmer, 1937. (M 220 L825P)

11. Poem for orchestra. New York: G. Schirmer, 1923. (M 1002 L825po)

12. Quatre Melodies pour chant et piano. New York: G. Schirmer, 1903.
      (M 1621 L825m)

13. Quintett in One Movement for three violins, viola and violoncello. New York:
      G. Schirmer, 1938. Score (M 552 L825Qs); Parts (M 552 L825Qp)

14. Serenade pour voix, alto et piano. New York: G. Schirmer, 1904.
      (M 1621.3 L825p)

Records

Title	Recording	ESM No.
1. Music for Four Stringed Instruments (Coolidge)	Vic M-543	A 326
2. A Pagan Poem, Op. 14 (E-R Orchestra)	Vic M-876 Cap P-8188	A 328 LP
3. String Quartet (Gordon)	Sch Set-13	A 327
4. Two Rhapsodies, Op. 5 (Piano, violin, oboe) a. The Pool b. The Bagpipe	Sch Set-10	A 325

II. Charles Tomlinson Griffes (1884-1920)

A. Life
   1. Born September 17, 1884, in Elmira, New York. Studied with local
      teachers; organist at the Lutheran Church. Studied piano and compo-
      sition in Berlin (1903-1907); had a few lessons with Humperdinck;
      composed songs, a string quartet, suite for string orchestra, over-
      ture for orchestra.
   2. Returned to America in 1907 and became an instructor in music at the
      Hackley School for boys in Tarrytown, N. Y. (1907-20). Played piano
      in first American performance of Stravinsky's Petrouchka (1916).
B. Music
   1. Griffes's compositions include principally songs and piano pieces
      (one sonata). He also wrote one symphonic work for large orchestra

and some chamber music.
  2. Five sets of teaching pieces and a few songs were published under the name of Arthur Tomlinson.
C. Style
  1. German influence (1907-1910) in early works (1907-1910).
    a. Five German Poems. Use of diatonic melodic lines; added sixths.
  2. Influence of French impressionism, oriental and exotic music (1910-1917).
    a. The Lake at Evening, Op. 5, No. 1 (1915)
      1) Impressionistic style; use of rhythmic pedal figure; augmented chords, chromatically added and altered tones.
    b. Roman Sketches, for piano, Op. 7 (1915-16); The White Peacock; Nightfall; The Fountains of the Acqua Paola (pentatonic scale, p. 1); Clouds (chromatic scale, meas. 12).
      1) The White Peacock (arr. for orchestra by the composer). Use of cross-rhythms; bitonality; alternating rhythms (3/2, 5/4, 7/4, 5/4); 7th, 9th, 11th chords; chromatic scale lines (meas. 3). The first section makes unusual use of dominant and second-dominant harmony in a basic E Major tonality.
    c. The Pleasure Dome of Kubla Khan
      1) Composed as a piano piece (1912), scored for orchestra (1916), revised by Frederick Stock (1919).
      2) A descriptive tone-poem based on the poem, Kubla Khan or A Vision in a Dream by Coleridge. Griffes used the section describing the stately palace: "the sunny pleasure-dome with caves of ice, the miracle of rare device."
      3) Many impressionistic devices and oriental-type themes are used.
      4) The work is scored for 3 flutes, 2 oboes, English horn, 2 clarinets in A, bass clarinet in B^b, 4 horns, 3 trumpets, 3 trombones, tuba, timpani, bass drum, cymbals, tambourine, gong, piano, celesta, 2 harps and strings.
      5) Introduction (meas. 1-15)
        a) Sacred Alph river and ice caverns.
      6) Part I (meas. 16-43)
        a) Palace gardens and fountains appear.
      7) Part II (meas. 47-138)
        a) Suggestions of revelry are heard.
      8) Part III (meas. 139-209)
        a) The dancing and revelry reach a climax.
      9) Coda (meas. 210-220)
        a) Return to the first mood.
  3. Strong influence of Orientalism
    a. Five Poems of Ancient China and Japan (1917)
    b. Two Sketches for String Quartet, based on Indian themes (1916-17)
  4. Late works
    a. Mark a turning away from impressionism and programmatic writing. The influence of Scriabin is apparent, however, and modern harmonic devices appear. Some influence of orientalism is still found.
    b. Sonata for Piano (Dec. 1918-Jan. 1918)
      1) Three movements (the first two are connected); cyclical form.
      2) First movement (Feroce-Allegretto con moto)
        a) Based on an oriental-sounding artificial scale (F-G#-A-B^b-C#-D-E^b)
        b) Sonata-allegro form: Introduction (meas. 1-8); Theme I (meas. 9-26); Theme II (meas. 24-47). Development (meas. 48-79). Recapitulation (meas. 80).
        c) Basic chord built in fourths (F-B^b-E^b)
      3) Second movement (Molto tranquillo)
        a) A (meas. 1-36) - B (meas. 37-49) - A (meas. 50-56) - Coda.
        b) Use of plainsong-like theme; polytonal effects; harsh dis-

cords.
    4) Third movement (Allegro vivace)
        a) A (meas. 1-42) - B (meas. 43-68) - A (meas. 69-125) - Coda
           for the entire sonata (meas. 126-223).
        b) Frequent changes of time signatures; use of polyrhythms;
           chords in fifths ($Bb-(D)-F\#-C\#$).
        c) Return of material from earlier movements.
  c. Poem for flute and orchestra (1918-1919)
    1) Written for Georges Barrère; scored for solo flute, 2 horns in
      E, snare drum, harp, strings. Published in arrangement for
      flute and piano.
    2) Use of modes.

BIBLIOGRAPHY

Books

1. Bauer, M.   Twentieth Century Music. New York: Putnam's Sons,
    1947. (ML 197 B344t)

2. Davies, K. C.   Charles Tomlinson Griffes and His Music. ESM Thesis,
    1937.

3. Howard, J. T.   Charles Tomlinson Griffes. New York: G. Schirmer,
    1923. (ML 410 G849H)

4. Maisel, E. M.   Charles T. Griffes. New York: A. Knopf, 1943.
    (ML 410 G849M23)

Periodicals

1. Bauer, M.   "Charles T. Griffes as I Remember Him," MQ XXIX
    (1943), 355.

2. Bauer, M.   "Impressionists in America," MM IV (Jan.-Feb, 1927),
    15.

3. Engel, C.   "Views and Reviews," MQ XXIX (1943), 405.

4. Peterkin, N.   "Charles T. Griffes," Chesterian (March, 1923), 131.

5. Rosenfeld, P.   "Griffes on Grand Street," MM XVIII (1940), 27.

6. Rudhyar, D.   "Griffes, Master of the Lied," Singing (June, 1927),
    24.

7. Upton, W. T.   "The Songs of C. T. Griffes," MQ IX (1923), 314.

Music

1. Clouds, Op. 7, No. 4, for piano. New York: G. Schirmer, 1917. (M 25 G849R)

2. Fantasy Pieces, Op. 6, for piano. New York: G. Schirmer, 1915. (M 25 G849F)

3. Five Poems of Ancient China and Japan, Op. 10, for medium voice and piano.
    New York: G. Schirmer, 1917. (M 1621 G849f)

4. Five German Poems for voice and piano. New York: G. Schirmer, 1909.
    (M 1621 G849G)

5. The Lake at Evening, Op. 5, No. 1, for piano. New York: G. Schirmer, 1915.

(M 21 R29Av.1)

6. The Pleasure-Dome of Kubla Khan. Revised by F. A. Stock. New York: G.
        Schirmer, 1929. (M 1002 G849pS)

7. Poem for flute and orchestra. New York: G. Schirmer, 1951. (M 1020 G849pS)

8. Roman Sketches, Op. 7, for the pianoforte. New York: G. Schirmer, 1917.
        (M 25 G849R)

9. Two Sketches for string quartet (based on Indian themes). New York: G.
        Schirmer, 1922. (M 452 G849S)

10. Sonata for piano. New York: G. Schirmer, 1921. (M 23 G849)

11. Symphony in Yellow, Op. 3, No. 2, for mezzo-soprano and piano. New York: G.
        Schirmer, 1915. (M 1621 G849t)

12. The White Peacock (arr. for orchestra). New York: G. Schirmer, 1945.
        (M 1145 G849W)

13. By a Lonely Forest Pathway, for voice and piano. New York: G. Schirmer, 19
        1909. (M 1621 G849g)

14. The Fountain of the Acqua Paola, Op. 7, No. 3, for piano. New York: G.
        Schirmer, 1917. (M 25 G849R)

15. Night Winds, Op. 5, No. 3, for piano. New York: G. Schirmer, 1915.
        (M 25 G849ni)

16. Three Poems by Fiona MacLeod, Op. 11, for voice and piano. New York: G.
        Schirmer, 1918. (M 1621 G849S)

17. Tone-Images, Op. 3, for voice and piano. New York: G. Schirmer, 1915.
        (M 1621 G849t)

18. The Vale of Dreams, Op. 5, No. 2, for piano. New York: G. Schirmer, 1915.
        (M 25 G849t.2)

Records

Title		Recording	ESM No.
1. By a Lonely Forest Pathway	(Darwin)	Vic 36224	R 624
	(Steber)	Vic 101071	R 1380
2. Pleasure Dome of Kubla Khan		Vic 7957	R 89
3. Poem for Flute and Orchestra (Baker and Saidenberg)		Dec DL-4013	LP 1443
	(Kincaid and Philadelphia)	Col ML-4629	LP 975
4. Roman Sketches, Op. 7 (Hambro)		Wald W-100	LP 642
a. The White Peacock			
b. Nightfall			
c. The Fountain of Acqua Paola			
d. Clouds			
5. Sonata for piano (Hambro)		Wald W-100	LP 642
	(Behrend)	All 3024	LP 69

6. Two Sketches for Strings Based on Indian   Vic 15417   R 530
    Themes (Coolidge)   Vic M-558   A 303

7. The White Peacock (arr. for orchestra)   Vic 15659   R 19
    (E-R Orchestra)   Vic M-608   A 1137
    (Barlow)   Col 17140   R 544

III. Daniel Gregory Mason (1873-1953)

    A. Life
        1. Born in Brookline, Massachusetts, November 20, 1873. He was a
            grandson of Lowell Mason and a nephew of William Mason. His father,
            Henry Mason, was one of the founders of the Mason and Hamlin piano
            company. Studied some with Ethelbert Nevin; was a student at Har-
            vard of John K. Paine (whose lectures he found dull), receiving his
            B.A. degree in 1895. Later studied with Whiting, Chadwick, Goet-
            schius; went to Paris in 1901 and studied with Vincent D'Indy.
        2. Appointed to music faculty of Columbia University in 1909 and in
            1929 became the MacDowell Professor of Music. Retired as head of the
            Department of Music in 1940 and was succeeded by Douglas Moore.
            Mason lectured extensively and was the author of many books. Re-
            ceived awards from the Juilliard Foundation and the Society for the
            Publication of American Music.
    B. Style
        1. Mason believed that American music is "necessarily eclectic and
            cosmopolitan; that its distinctiveness must be individual, rather
            than national." He was in no sense revolutionary and preferred the
            classic-romantic principles and forms of Beethoven, Schumann,
            Brahms, and Franck. In regard to originality he stated: "Be original
            at your peril; if you wish immediate popularity, you must imitate
            current models." He wrote with sincerity and his craftsmanship is of
            the highest order. Many of his early works were revised for later
            publication.
        2. Although he considered himself a conservative, he was not unaware of
            the trends of his time. He made some use of the whole-tone scale,
            triads with the added sixth, suggestions of polytonality, parallel
            open fifths, and tone clusters of consecutive chromatic chords.
        3. The classic forms of the Sonata-Allegro, Fugue, Variation are used.
        4. Borrowed themes are found in the Quartet on Negro Themes ("Deep
            River" and others); Serenade for Quartet ("Fanny Blair"); Suite after
            English Folk Songs and other works.
        5. Cyclic treatment is found in the Symphonies and descriptive titles in
            the Lincoln Symphony.

BIBLIOGRAPHY

Books

1. The Appreciation of Music Series. 5. vols. New York: H. W. Gray Co., 1909.
        (MT 6 S961)

2. The Art of Music. New York: The National Society of Music, 1915-1916.
        (ML 100 M39)

3. Artistic Ideals. New York: W. W. Norton & Co., 1927. (ML 60 M39a)

4. Beethoven and His Forerunners. New York: The Macmillan Co., 1930.
        (ML 390 M39.3)

5. The Chamber Music of Brahms. New York: The Macmillan Co., 1933.

(MT 145 B81M39)

6. <u>A Child's Guide to Music</u>. New York: The Baker and Taylor Co., 1909.
     LP 3930 M39)

7. <u>Contemporary Composers</u>. New York: The Macmillan Co., 1918. (ML 390 M39C)

8. <u>The Dilemma of American Music</u>, <u>and Other Essays</u>. New York: The Macmillan
     Co., 1928. (ML 60 M39d)

9. <u>From Grieg to Brahms</u>. New York: The Outlook Co., 1902, 1927. (ML 390 M39f)
     (ML 390 M39f.2)

10. <u>From Song to Symphony</u>. Boston: Oliver Ditson Co., 1924. (MT 6 M398f)

11. <u>A Guide to Music, for Beginners and Others</u>. Garden City: Doubleday, Page
     and Co., 1913. (ML 3930 M398g)

12. <u>Music and the Plain Man</u>. New York: H. W. Gray Co., 1924. (ML 3975 M399m)

13. <u>Music in My Time and Other Reminiscences</u>. New York: The Macmillan Co., 1938.
     (ML 410 M399m)

14. <u>A Neglected Sense in Piano-Playing.</u> New York: G. Schirmer, 1912. (MT 220
     (MT 220 M399)

15. <u>The Orchestral Instruments and What They Do</u>. New York: H. W. Gray Co., 1909.
     (MT 90 M39.1)

16. <u>The Quartets of Beethoven</u>. New York: Oxford University Press, 1947.
     (MT 145 B41M398)

17. <u>Reading with a Purpose</u>. Chicago: American Library Assn., 1925. (MT 6 M398r)

18. <u>The Romantic Composers</u>. New York: The Macmillan Co., 1926. (ML 390 M39r)

19. <u>Tune in America</u>. New York: A. A. Knopf, 1931. (ML 200.5 M398)

<u>Periodicals</u>

1. Thompson, R.   "The Contemporary Scene in American Music," <u>MQ</u> XVIII
     (1932), 13.

2. Tuthill, B. C.   "Daniel Gregory Mason," <u>MQ</u> XXXIV (1948), 46.

<u>Articles by D. G. Mason</u>

3. "Artistic Ideals - Universality," <u>MQ</u> XII (1926), 1.

4. "Artistic Ideals - Workmanship," <u>MQ</u> XII (1926), 481.

5. "Artistic Ideals - Originality," <u>MQ</u> XIII (1927), 1.

6. "Artistic Ideals - Universality," <u>MQ</u> XIII (1927), 345.

7. "The Artist and His Fellows," <u>ML</u> VII (1926), 246.

8. "Brahms Third Symphony," <u>MQ</u> XVII (1931), 374.

9. "A Conservative Composer's Confession of Artistic Faith," <u>New York Times</u>
     (April 4, 1948)

10. "Dictator Conductors," <u>Am</u>. <u>Scholar</u> (Oct., 1941), 447.

11. "A Glimpse of Lowell Mason," <u>NMR</u> (Jan., 1927), 49.

12. "The Masons: Cultural Pioneers," <u>Mus</u>. <u>Digest</u> (Dec., 1946), 10.

13. "Memories of William Mason," <u>The</u> <u>Etude</u> (Sept., 1936), 543.

14. "A Pragmatic Review of Harmony, <u>NMR</u> (April, 1911), 242; (May, 1911), 306.

15. "What Do We Mean by Classic?" <u>The</u> <u>Etude</u> (Dec., 1932), 845.

Music

A. <u>Orchestral</u>

1. <u>Symphony No. 1 in C minor</u>, Op. 11 (1913-14; rev. 1922). New York: Universal Edition, 1925. (M 1001 M398)

2. <u>Chanticleer</u>, Festival Overture, Op. 27 (1926). Boston: C. C. Birchard, 1928. (M 1004 M399C)

3. <u>Prelude and Fugue</u> for piano and orchestra, Op. 20 (1919). New York: J. Fischer, 1933. (M 215 M398p)

4. <u>Suite after English Folk Songs</u>, Op. 32 (1933-34). New York: G. Schirmer, 1936. (M 1003 M398)

5. <u>Symphony No. 3 (A Lincoln Symphony)</u>, Op. 35 (1935-36). New York: Juilliard, 1944. (M 1001 M398.3)

B. <u>Chamber</u>

6. <u>Sonata in G minor</u> for violin and piano, Op. 5 (1907-8; rev. 1944). New York: G. Schirmer, 1944. (M 219 M399)

7. <u>Three Pieces</u> for flute, harp and string quartet, Op. 13 (1911-12; rev. 1943). New York: Society for the Publication of American Music, 1943. (M 682 M39)

8. <u>Sonata</u> for clarinet, (or violin), and piano, Op. 14 (1912-15; rev. 1945). New York: Society for the Publication of American Music, 1946. (M 250 M39)

9. <u>Intermezzo</u> for string quartet, Op. 17 (1916; rev. 1937). New York: Weaner-Levant, 1943. (M 452 M398I)

10. <u>Variations on a Theme of John Powell</u> for string quartet, Op. 24 (1924-25). New York: Carl Fischer, 1928. I(M 452 M398v)

11. <u>String Quartet on Negro Themes</u>, Op. 19 (1918-19; rev. 1930). New York: Society for the Publication of American Music, 1930. (M 452 M398q)

12. <u>Fanny Blair</u>, <u>Folk-Song Fantasy</u> for string quartet, Op. 28 (1927). New York: Carl Fischer, 1930. (M 452 M398F)

13. <u>Serenade</u> for string quartet, Op. 31 (1931). New York: Society for the Publication of American Music, 1934. (M 452 M398s)

14. <u>Sentimental Sketches for violin</u>, cello, piano, Op. 34. New York: J. Fischer, 1935. (M 312 M398s)

C. Piano

   15. Birthday Waltzes, Op. 1 (1894; rev. 1923). Boston: E. C. Schirmer, 1923.
      (M 32 M398b)

   16. Three Silhouettes, Op. 21 (1921). New York: G. Schirmer, 1923. (M 25
      (M 25 M398s)

   17. Divertimento for two pianos, Op. 26A (1926). New York: Carl Fischer,
      1927. (M 215 M398d)

   18. Three Preludes, Op. 33. New York: E. B. Marks, 1943. (M 25 M398pr)

D. Organ

   19. Passacaglia and Fugue, Op. 10 (1912). New York: H. W. Gray, 1913.

   20. Two Chorale-Preludes on Hymn Tunes, Op. 30 (1941). New York: J. Fischer,
      1942.

E. Voice

   21. Four Songs, Op. 4 (1896) (Mary L. Mason). Philadelphia: John Church,
      1908. (M 1619 C56v.3)

   22. Three Songs (from "Nautical Lays of a Landsman"), Op. 38 (1943) (Wallace
      Irwin). New York: G. Schirmer, 1943. (M 1621 M398s)

   23. When First My Way to Fair I Took (A. E. Housman). New York: M. Witmark
      and Sons, 1936. (M 1621 M398W)

Records

Title	Recording	ESM No.
1. Quartet in G minor on Negro Themes, Op. 19 (Coolidge)	Vic M-891	A 371
2. The Whippoorwill (from "Country Pictures") (Behrend)	Vic M-764	A 939
		A 1435

INDEX